Jung, Synchronicity, and
Human Destiny

Jung, Synchronicity, and Human Destiny

C. G. Jung's Theory of
Meaningful Coincidence

by IRA PROGOFF

Julian
Press

Copyright © 1973 by Ira Progoff
Published by The Julian Press, Inc., a member of the Crown
Publishing Group, 225 Park Avenue South, New York, New York
10003
JULIAN PRESS and colophon are trademarks of Crown Publishers,
Inc.

Manufactured in the United States of America

Library of Congress Cataloging-in-Publication Data

Progoff, Ira.
    Jung, synchronicity, and human destiny.

    Previously published under title: Jung, synchronicity & human
destiny. 1973.
    Bibliography: p.
    1. Jung, C. G. (Carl Gustav), 1875–1961—Views on coincidence.
2. Coincidence.   I. Title.
BF173.J85P68   1987   150.19′54   87-3250
ISBN 0-517-56636-2

10 9 8 7 6 5 4 3 2
1987 First paperback edition

Contents

Jung, Synchronicity, and
Human Destiny

I Interpreting the Multiple Universe: Jung and Teilhard de Chardin

One of the great expectations that the nineteenth century bequeathed to us was its confidence that the methods of the physical sciences would succeed equally well in the study of man. That hope, of course, has not materialized. During the past generation it has become necessary to reconsider some of the fundamental conceptions of science in order to open the way for a larger, more balanced perspective. It has become clear that the early optimism reflected the excitement and exuberance of the day when the scientific method was first demonstrating how successful it could be. That was the enthusiasm of youth, and the time has come now for the considered reflections of maturity.

As we recognize that there are many sides to the universe, we realize that each of these dimensions may require an interpretive principle capable of reflecting the special qualities inherent in it. The complexity of an infinite universe may well require a number of interpretive principles at the basic levels where under-

1

standing is to be achieved. This possibility is the starting point for the inquiry described in this book. It is the large and general perspective in which we examine principles that are alternatives to causality, specifically Jung's hypothesis of the principle of *Synchronicity* as an addition and complement to the laws of cause and effect.

Many people have experienced a deep disappointment in realizing that the human mind and the destiny of the individual life cannot be reduced to the same type of causal laws that have been the basic tools of natural science. Students of psychology and society have reluctantly acknowledged that approaches that had been so impressively productive in other areas of research would not necessarily be applicable for them. This lack has left a vacuum in many areas of the study of man, but new suggestions are being raised, oddly enough, in the very fields where science has been most successful. During the past generation the advance of theoretical physics has led to the recognition that there is an open, indeterminate factor at work even in the physical universe, and that the element of contingency is large enough to require significant modifications in the principle of causality. In place of the absolute and dogmatic faith that the nineteenth century placed in causality, there is now arising a new skepticism, and an awareness that the entire range of issues must be critically reappraised.

Many have come to realize that the one-sidedness of rationalism is less an expression of the scientific attitude than of an outworn faith in a narrow version of

2

science. That this faith is begetting its own skepticism is comparable in many ways to the development of a skeptical attitude among the early scientists in rejecting the religious faiths of the Middle Ages. It also is opening the way for basic new conceptions. Now, science is no longer being conceived in the terms of a restrictive rationalism, but is understood in the full generic meaning of the word *science,* as knowing, as man's total quest for knowledge. Thus, modern science is increasingly free of the inhibitions that the intellectual Victorianism of the rationalistic mind imprinted on it. The new exploratory freedom is making it possible to approach the phenomena of the universe from a much broader vantage point.

In this spirit, on the basis of a hunchlike intuition that there is a correspondence, or at least a parallel, between the work of theoretical physics and his own researches in depth psychology, Jung began to formulate in the latter nineteen-twenties the principle of "acausal relationship," which he named *Synchronicity.*

The concept of Synchronicity was originally suggested to him by his observations in studying the deep levels of the Self, especially as he noted the correlation between the movement of events within dreams and the style of interpretation that he found in certain ancient, especially oriental, scriptures and commentaries with respect to changes of destiny in the course of a human life. The immediate impetus to formulate the details of his hypothesis, however, came from his contact with the physicists Nils Bohr and Wolfgang

Pauli and from his early friendship with Albert Einstein. In the course of his discussions with them, he noted the equivalence of the atom as the basic unit of the physical world and the psyche of the human being. The correspondence is especially strong when the atom is compared to the conception of the psyche that Jung had developed as his distinctive approach to the depths of man.

Noting the similarity, the idea came to Jung that, if great sums of energy could be released by breaking the elemental unit of the atom, equivalent sums of energy might be brought forth if the depths of the psyche could be opened in a comparable way. This was the great hunch and hypothesis that led him to carry his explorations into many unconventional areas. We are now able to see the relevance of what he was doing, but during the second quarter of this century, when Jung was conducting his main investigations, the fields of study to which his hunches led him seemed outlandish indeed.

One primary result of Jung's researches in areas that his contemporaries rejected and ridiculed is the conception of Synchronicity. He presented it as a means of filling a gap in the world view of science, specifically as a balance to the principle of causality. One distinguishing quality of Synchronicity, however, is that it includes nonphysical as well as physical phenomena, and that it perceives these in *noncausal but meaningful* relationship to one another. As we proceed, we shall see the numerous and subtle overlays of meaning that are contained in this statement. The

4

heart of the matter, however, is that Jung was engaged in working out a principle of interpretation that would make it possible to comprehend phenomena in which the psyche of man is involved at deeper than conscious levels.

Jung himself does not refer to Pierre Teilhard de Chardin in this respect, but Teilhard's cosmology of evolution provides a perspective in which we can see the significance of the *Synchronicity* hypothesis in the larger framework of life.

In Teilhard's schematic view, the process of evolution proceeds through a succession of spheres culminating in the *Noosphere*. He marks off a number of successive stages in the evolutionary process, which he also describes as "zones" or "spheres." Thus Teilhard lists the *barysphere,* the *lithosphere,* the *hydrosphere,* the *atmosphere,* the *stratosphere,* the *biosphere,* and ultimately the *noosphere.* The primary characteristic of these spheres within the perspective of Teilhard's thought is their relation to the emergence of life, and to the further development of life in the spirit of man. Thus the first stages that he describes refer to the condition of the universe before life has evolved. The emergence of life carries the evolution of the universe forward to a significantly higher level. The *biosphere,* in Teilhard's formulation, contains all the expressions of life in both its plant and animal forms. It is at this level, the level of the *biosphere,* that the human species emerges, and with it a radically transforming factor enters the evolution of the universe. The life of man brings forth *mind,* and eventually the creative

5

products of the *spirit*. From these a further realm is formed that is a qualitatively higher level of evolution. This is the *Noosphere*, the sphere of spirit and meaning, which opens before us now as the great potential of human existence.

The Noosphere is the dimension of reality in which the special quality of human life is expressed. Teilhard's description of it is more visionary and impressionistic than literal, but the conception he has in mind is definite nonetheless, and is rich with suggestive implications. In Teilhard's vision of it, the Noosphere is a layer of reality, or "envelop" as he describes it, that surrounds the physical earth as an atmosphere. It is an envelop around the physical, but it itself is not physical. It may be conceived of as being composed of particles of human consciousness. In a manner of speaking, these are the sparks that rise up from the experiences of the human psyche. Thus the Noosphere was not in existence before man came upon the evolutionary scene. Its contents are derived from man's cumulative life. They are formed by the inner experiences of mankind, especially those that take place at the depth level of consciousness. In this sense, the development of the Noosphere is an emergent of human life, and especially of the further evolution of man in terms of the interior dimension of his existence.

Since the Noosphere, as the emergent dimension of man in evolution is qualitatively different in its content from that of the spheres that came before it, we can infer that the principles by which it can be understood and interpreted may also be different. The laws of cause and effect may possibly be sufficient to understand the operation of those laws that govern the operation of the universe at the stages before life emerged. These causal laws, together with the principles of organic teleology, may at a further level be sufficient to enable us to understand and interpret the processes that operate on the level of the universe where life, as plant and animal, is present, as on the level of the *biosphere*. But something additional is present in the *Noosphere*; and there is reason to infer, if we follow Teilhard's general conception, that an interpretive principle in addition to causality and organic teleology is required in order to comprehend the nature of the events that take place within it.[1]

Teilhard does not himself make this point with respect to the interpretive principles that apply to each of the major spheres that he describes; and Jung does not acknowledge the validity of Teilhard's systematic conception of levels of evolution. Setting the two side by side, however, has the effect of adding a dimension of meaning to each of them. From one side, Teilhard's perspective presents a framework in which we see the larger evolutionary significance of the Synchronicity concept. From the other side, the very conception of the Noosphere implies the need of a special principle with which to comprehend the events taking place in it. Teilhard does not supply

[1] Pierre Teilhard de Chardin. *The Phenomenon of Man*. Translated by Bernard Wall. New York: Harper & Brothers, 1959.

this, since his description of the Noosphere is primarily intuitive. It is clear that, according to his understanding, the *envelop of Noosphere* is progressively formed by individual events taking place at the depth of the psyche in the course of human experiences. But Teilhard himself does not enter into the question of what factors at the depth of the psyche bring the contents of the Noosphere into existence. Neither does Teilhard open the question of what interpretative principle might enable us to comprehend the mode of functioning within the Noosphere.

Jung's work provides specific hypotheses that enable us to conceive the nature of the events by which the Noosphere is built. Jung did not by any means foresee this role for his conception of Synchronicity, but one of its important contributions is bound to be that it helps fill out the new and expanding view of the universe that is exemplified in authors like Teilhard de Chardin. Jung does this in two specific ways that we shall see in detail as we proceed in our discussion of Synchronicity. The first is that, with his theory of the archetypal factors operating at the depth of the psyche, and especially his description of the numerous powers and energies they contain, Jung provides a means of understanding the nature of the human experiences that form the Noosphere. The second is that with his interpretative principle of Synchronicity, he gives us a tangible means for exploring the elusive ways in which, out of the depth of the psyche, events and awarenesses of special significance are brought into existence.

8

We thus receive from Jung two very seminal hypotheses with respect firstly to the contents and secondly to the principle of operation of the Noosphere. When we translate Teilhard's phrase into the terms of its more general significance and see it as the front edge of evolution emerging from the experiences of the human spirit, the mutual support of Jung and Teilhard de Chardin becomes clear. Both are contributors to the new world view that is taking shape in this generation. Teilhard's view of spiritual evolution expands the perspective of time; and within that context, the Synchronicity principle can play an important role both as an hypothesis for science and as a way of experience at the frontal edge of life where further evolution is occurring.

II Synchronicity, Science, and the Esoteric

The contexts in which Jung discusses the principle of Synchronicity provide an interesting combination of opposites. On the one hand, he places his discussions within the framework of theoretical physics, relating it to the reconsideration by many scientists of the validity of causality as the exclusive interpretive principle. On the other hand, he refers to various esoteric and occult teachings of prescientific times as indicators of man's intuitive recognition of the presence of the Synchronicity principle in the universe. These two sources of data, the rational scientific and the non-rational esoteric, may seem to be in conflict, but they are not contradictory. They are two sides of a single reality, and one of Jung's purposes is to enable us to see their common quality and their relation to each other.

An effect, however, of Jung's drawing such disparate materials together in one discussion is that his theories became suspect as well as confusing to more conventional minds. Given the atmosphere of thought during the past three decades, this is one of the main reasons why Synchronicity has received scant attention until now.

All through the years when he was developing his major and fundamental theories, Jung drew on pre-scientific intuitive systems of thought as sources of data for his psychological understanding. By doing this, he repeatedly scandalized those who thought of themselves as being more "scientific" than he. He was merely availing himself of additional sources of information; but those who did not understand what he was trying to do thought he was being unscientific. An example of this is the introduction that Jung wrote to the new edition of the *I Ching* in 1949. There, in suggesting a basis for the uncanny results that the procedures of the *I Ching* often achieve, he referred to Synchronicity as an interpretative principle that enables us to understand how the oracles, or predictive readings, of the *I Ching* operate. He was presenting it as a general principle that has its relevance in the field of physics as well, but we can see how such discussions limited the consideration he could receive in scientific circles.

Another example of this occurred when Jung was writing his basic presentation of Synchronicity in what became the only full-length book he devoted to it. In the course of this, he set up an experiment designed to demonstrate the presence of Synchronicity with statistical evidence. The difficulty with the experiment, however, was that he set it up in terms of the relationship between the astrological signs of married couples. This type of "experiment" was also bound to be unconvincing. It turned out, as we shall see later in our discussion, to be unconvincing not only to the scientifically minded because of its astrological contents, but to the mathematicians who rejected the statistical material as well. These are instances of the not infrequent times when Jung's style of presentation placed hurdles in the path of the theories for which he was seeking support. Especially in the case of Synchronicity, which is an hypothesis that has a general meaning much beyond the categories into which astrology and the *I Ching* are conventionally placed, Jung's presentation was subject to misinterpretation from the beginning.

It is a fact nonetheless that Synchronicity has a significant contribution to make in clarifying and giving us insight into various approaches to human experience like astrology and the *I Ching*. These approaches have been held suspect by the modern mind since they cannot be understood in "the dry light of science." They are in fact not "dry" (in the pre-Socratic sense of "wet souls") but wet with the waters that flow at the deep levels of the psyche. Jung's interest in various types of esoteric teachings and methods has been based on his insight that, in some obscure way, they express the "underside" of human experiences. They are not to be taken literally, but like dreams, should be given an opportunity to speak for themselves within the context of their own indigenous symbolism. Jung truly undertook to give the esoteric and the occult an opportunity to speak and reveal each its special style of wisdom. He did this with interpretations and introductions to books on these subjects, ranging literally from *A* to *Z*, from Alchemy to Zen; and in between were Astrology, the *Book of the Dead*, the Tarot, the *I Ching*, and many others drawn from ancient, Eastern, and primitive cultures.

All these teachings and methods were "true" in Jung's eyes in the sense that they carried a perception of reality drawn from the nonconscious and intuitive levels of the psyche. They were not "true in themselves" in the sense of being descriptions of external reality to be taken literally. But they were descriptions of the interior landscape, and to that degree were true as symbolic perceptions of a dimension of reality that can be reached only indirectly.

In saying this, we come to the fundamental awareness in Jung's work that enables him to deal with "psychological facts" without making them "nothing but" psychological. There is a dimension of human experience that is not external to us in the sense that it can be directly and tangibly grasped. Rather, it is within us, but the word *within* must also be understood metaphorically.[1] It reflects a depth in us as human beings and also a depth of the universe. Perceiving one, we perceive the other. But we cannot do

---

[1] The anonymous fourteenth-century monk who wrote *The Cloud of Unknowing* understood this point well. We may find God by looking upward, but not necessarily physically upward. This indirect symbolic perception he called "spiritually knowing." See *The Cloud of Unknowing*, translation with commentary by Ira Progoff. New York: Julian Press, 1957. Delta Paperback, 1973.

13

so directly, as we would in laying our hands on something and grasping it. We can only do so indirectly,
or symbolically.

This is the essence of the esoteric and occult teachings and methods of the past. They are indirect and
symbolic perceptions of a dimension of reality that
can be reached in no other way. People who do not
understand this and take those teachings at face value
miss the point altogether, and therefore they think
that these approaches are nothing but superstitions.
They are not superstitions at all, *unless* they are taken
literally by those who *believe* in them. Then they become dogmatic truths, and with that they become un-
true to the larger truth they are reflecting. When they
are hardened, externalized, and treated as *the* way,
they do tend to degenerate into superstitions. As long
as they remain fluid, however, they are like deep
dreams and myths that provide a living connection to
the elusive and transpersonal reality of the universe.
Then the symbolism of each provides *a* way. While
none is literally true in itself, all are true in some
form and in some degree as paradoxical *vehicles*
traveling toward a place of spirit that can only be
reached indirectly.

Jung wished to indicate the important contribution that such esoteric teachings can make to our
understanding of the elusive but fundamental realities of human existence. That was why he intro-
duced so many of them to the Western public, and
left himself open to scorn for doing so. There was,
however, more than general reason for Jung's dealing

with esoteric materials in his discussions of Synchronicity. He perceived a specific twofold connection between them. On the one hand, the *I Ching* brings
about a type of experience that provides valuable il-
lustrative data in explaining the hypothesis of Synchronicity. On the other hand, the formulation of the
Synchronicity principle provides a specific tool with
which the intuitive wisdom of many esoteric texts
may be entered and comprehended more profoundly.
Synchronicity can become a master key for opening
the door to teachings regarding the nature of human
destiny that have heretofore been closed to us. In this
regard Synchronicity has the special merit of being
not only a key to the occult dimension of life, but a
key that has the experience of modern science behind it.

When Jung began to present his idea of Synchronicity in his writings, he wished to indicate its relation to the various esoteric traditions. At the same
time, recognizing the intellectual atmosphere in the
midst of which he was speaking, he knew that he had
to keep his concepts as separate as possible from asso-
ciations that would cause them to be rejected. Para-
doxically, it is this desire to help his concepts gain
acceptance that accounts in large measure for the ambiguity that is often found in Jung's work, and that
has delayed its acceptance. In his writings there is an
alternation of strongly forthright statements followed
by modifications and disclaimers that have the effect
of softening the impact of his points.

It often seems as though, having fearlessly rushed

out ahead of his time, he sought as an afterthought to protect himself by hedging his position with statements that neutralized the thrust of what he had said. He apparently often had reason to feel that he was not being understood. An example of this hedging in another area of Jung's work occurs in his famous Terry Lectures on *Psychology and Religion* given in 1937.[1] There, while demonstrating the importance and validity of religious experience, Jung also moved in the opposite direction in deference to the rationalism of his audience by saying that all he was doing was describing some phenomena of the human psyche. He was neutralizing the thrust of his work by bowing in the direction of the more conventional attitudes.

We often see it to be the case in history that great innovators cannot avoid paying "the penalty of taking the lead." Moving very far out in front makes them vulnerable and places them in positions that are easily misunderstood. This has been the case in several areas of Jung's work, particularly with respect to Synchronicity because of the nature of its material. We shall find it necessary to make allowances for the ambiguities and imbalances that arise because of this. But we can be assured that that effort will be well worth making, at least as much in the case of Synchronicity as has proven true in other areas of Jung's work.

[1] C. G. Jung. *Psychology and Religion*, Yale University Press, 1938, Vol. XI, in the Collected Works of C. G. Jung, Princeton, N.J.: Princeton University Press.

With this background, the present manuscript already has a long history behind it as it approaches publication in 1973. The central part of it, the primary expositions and interpretations, are drawn from a manuscript that was written in 1954 when I was engaged in a study of the advanced work of Jung's later years under a Bollingen fellowship.

That manuscript was the outcome of my studies with Jung at his home in Switzerland during the years 1952 and 1953. During 1954, after I had returned to the United States and had written my study of Synchronicity among other manuscripts dealing with his later work, our discussions continued through the mails. Jung became very much involved in the editing of the manuscript, especially since he was still working on the Synchronicity question with great intensity. At several points he wrote his comments into the manuscript. He inserted these comments in pencil, sometimes in the margins, sometimes between the lines, and sometimes extending his lengthier remarks across the backs of the preceding pages. Where they are relevant to our discussion, these comments in Jung's penciled longhand have been reproduced in this volume. Later, in 1955, I visited Jung again as part of my general study project, and this provided an opportunity to carry our discussions much further.

One of the questions we discussed in 1955 was of a practical nature. It involved the timing of the publication of the English translation of Jung's basic volume. My manuscript interpreting his theory of

Synchronicity had been based on my reading his text in the original German edition. In the meanwhile, an English translation was completed by R. F. C. Hull, and it was being prepared for publication in England. When the first galley sheets were ready, they were sent to me to assist in my commentaries. With their help, and with Jung's prompt responses, my Synchronicity manuscript progressed rapidly. But Jung's manuscript on which it was based ran into delays, primarily because certain minor statistical sections that had been included in the German version were being reviewed and altered for the English edition.

As time moved on, it became clear that it would be inappropriate to publish my interpretive book before the basic volume appeared in English. Publication was therefore postponed in 1955; and it was postponed again in 1956 when I became involved in other writings and activities. By that time, the response to the English publication of Jung's book and my own further considerations on the subject made it clear to me that there was still additional work to be done on the Synchronicity hypothesis. I therefore set my manuscript to one side; but I continued to study the subject in the midst of my other activities.

Over the years since that time, my projects and researches have enabled me to work with the Synchronicity concept in a variety of circumstances. It has consistently found a place, for example, in my practice of psychotherapy, in group workshops, in university seminars, in the Drew University Graduate Institute research on the lives of creative persons, and especially, since 1966, in the Dialogue House Intensive Journal program.

The last named has been especially rich as an empirical resource of Synchronicity experiences for two important reasons. The first is that its method of Journal keeping as a means of individual life development serves to accumulate a spontaneous record of synchronistic experiences that would otherwise tend to be ignored or forgotten. The second is that its procedures of *Journal Feedback* bring about a progressive deepening of the atmosphere both in the group workshops and in the private use of the *Intensive Journal*. This "deepening" increases the possibility of synchronistic experiences. Thus the Dialogue House work in personal growth has had an unplanned but significant by-product. It has demonstrated the presence of synchronistic events in the ordinary course of life experience, and this data has been preserved for research in various forms.

For this reason we have come to a further point in the type of research that is possible with respect to the Synchronicity hypothesis. Now that more factual data is available to us, Jung's concept can be taken as the starting point for further investigation and can be empirically tested with data drawn from everyday reality. To set a basis for this research is a primary reason for drawing out the 1954 essay on Synchronicity and making it available now in 1973 in a revised and enlarged form.

The original manuscript is the core of the present volume, especially with respect to the exposition of the basic concepts and particular points of interpretation. A substantial amount of material has been added, especially in integrating Jung's comments into the body of the text and in incorporating some of my observations of Synchronicity since the time of the original writing. After nineteen years, however, the primary purpose of this volume is still mainly preparatory. It is to describe and interpret Jung's conception of Synchronicity with respect to its larger philosophy and theoretical foundations, and to present the essence of this complicated matter as clearly as can be. In the course of these discussions, we shall also be preparing the way for a later consideration of the reformulations and shiftings of emphasis that may eventually be necessary in order to work with the Snychronicity hypothesis more productively. We thus have the ultimate goal that, when the Synchronicity concept has been clarified and appropriately reformulated, we will be able to use it as a hypothesis in studying the records of spontaneous experience that are now available to us.

In this context, Synchronicity is significant to us on two levels. On a theoretical level, it opens an additional dimension of consciousness with respect to the nature of human experience in the unfolding universe. And on the empirical level, it provides avenues for the factual study for some of the most elusive aspects of human life and destiny.

III Using the *I Ching* with Jung: A Personal Experience

Of all the esoteric methods that Jung studied, the *I Ching* is the clearest expression of the Synchronicity principle, and the one that applies it in the most sophisticated form. Jung had already known of the *I Ching* when he met the noted Sinologist, Richard Wilhelm, who was then engaged in making a major new translation of the *I Ching* into German. That translation has now established itself as the leading version, having been translated into English by Cary Baynes with an introduction by Jung.[1] Jung's association with Wilhelm was of major importance in the development of his conception of Synchronicity, for it gave him an opportunity to draw upon Wilhelm's knowledge of the noncausal sense of "patterning" that plays so important a role in ancient Chinese thinking. Jung's commentary on *The Secret of the Golden Flower*, a text of Chinese alchemy translated

[1] The *I Ching*, translated by Richard Wilhelm and Cary F. Baynes. Foreword by C. G. Jung. Bollingen Series XIX. Princeton, N.J.: Princeton University Press, 1950, 1969.

by Wilhelm, is also a product of this relationship. Jung's elaboration of that text is an important source for the development of some of the major psychological concepts of his later period. It is significant that Jung's first public use of the term "Synchronicity" occurred in the course of the eulogy he delivered at Richard Wilhelm's funeral in 1930.[1]

When the English version of the Wilhelm translation of the *I Ching* was being prepared in 1949, Jung wrote an introduction seeking to convey the spirit of its method to an unfriendly Western generation. In that introduction he gave a general statement of Synchronicity that can serve as a preliminary definition for our further discussion. He was speaking there of the basic method of the *I Ching*, to throw the coins six times and thus to form a pattern of odd and even, heads or tails, broken or unbroken lines. These lines form the hexagram that reflects the quality of the given moment of time at which the coins were thrown. The texts in the *I Ching* correspond to each of these hexagrams, sixty-four in all, and from these the individual draws the reading of the oracle referring to the elements of his destiny contained in that moment. The method is based upon the belief that the hexagram is "an indicator of the essential situation prevailing in the moment of its origin."

"This assumption," Jung continues, "involves a

---

[1] See C. G. Jung, "Richard Wilhelm: An Obituary" in *Collected Works,* Vol. XV. Originally published as the appendix to *The Secret of the Golden Flower* under the title, "In Memory of Richard Wilhelm." This memorial address was delivered in 1930.

certain curious principle that I have termed synchronicity, a concept that formulates a point of view diametrically opposed to that of causality. Since the latter is a merely statistical truth and not absolute, it is a sort of working hypothesis of how events evolve one out of another, whereas synchronicity takes the coincidence of events in space and time as meaning something more than mere chance, namely, a peculiar interdependence of objective events among themselves as well as with the subjective (psychic) states of the observer or observers."[1]

The central concept in that definition lies in the phrase, "Synchronicity takes the coincidence of events in space and time as meaning something more than mere chance." Perhaps a more indicative word than "coincidence" would be "cooccurrence," since the central thought concerns the occurrence at the same moment of two separate events that are not causally connected to one another. They take place at the same time with neither one having an effect on the other, and yet they are related to one another in a meaningful way. This is the principle that underlies the use of the *I Ching*. It calls upon two separate events occurring at a single moment and draws great meaning from them, even though there is no cause-and-effect relationship between the events.

Of the two events, one is the situation at a given moment in a person's life. The second event is the act of throwing the coins (or the yarrow stalks), with

[1] *I Ching,* op. cit.

the consequent reading of the *I Ching* text that the pattern of the coins calls up. Neither event has any apparent causal influence on the other. And yet almost invariably the readings of the text have an uncanny relevance for the life of the person.

As an illustration, let me tell my experience in using the *I Ching* twenty years ago with C. G. Jung in Switzerland.

At that time, I had just published my first book on Jung's work, and with the support of a Bollingen fellowship, I was studying with Jung, emphasizing the advanced concepts he had developed in his later years. That period was an open moment in my life. The opportunity to spend a considerable amount of time with him had come unexpectedly, and after a year in Europe the range of my researches under Jung's influence was becoming much deeper and broader.

One day in June of 1953 we were sitting in his garden beside the Lake of Zurich when he abruptly said to me, "Have you ever used the *I Ching?*"

"No," I said.

"Would you like to?"

"By all means."

"Well, then," he said, "let's do it."

He reached into his pocket and drew out a small, well-worn leather purse. It looked almost as old as he was. I had already had an opportunity to discover, on one occasion when I had used Jung's typewriter to prepare material we were working on, that he became attached to his possessions as old friends and tried to avoid giving them up. He liked new ideas and old

24

surroundings. That typewriter had been about as old as his purse. Now he opened the purse, drew out a handful of coins, and methodically sorted them out.

"Now we have it," he said, and handed me three Swiss dimes. "You can use my coins because you're here with me, but you have to throw them yourself."

We found a clear, flat place on the ground and I prepared to throw the three coins. Just before I threw them, Jung stopped me. "Wait," he said, "what question do you have?"

I took that to mean that I was to ask about a particular problem that was troubling me and for which I required an answer. The fact is that, for that interlude in my life when my research fellowship enabled me to work with Jung in Switzerland in that open relationship, I could not imagine any problems. It seemed to me that there were no clouds in the sky. Nonetheless there were numerous questions, some of them large questions, with respect to the eventual meaning of what I was doing, how it would proceed, and what my plans should be for the future. Thus I answered Jung that I had no specific problem to place before the *I Ching*. "But let's make it the situation as a whole," I said. "Let's make it the fact of my being here talking with you now."

Jung nodded and smiled. He seemed satisfied with my response. "Good," he said. When we discussed it later, he explained to me his views on the best way to use the *I Ching*, based on his experience with it. One important aspect, he said, is to place oneself as much as one can in the midst of the moment of time positioned at the center of the moment. We shall be able to understand more fully as we proceed with the discussion of Synchronicity why this is of especial practical value in using the *I Ching*. It makes it possible for the entire moment of the present to express itself, and to include in its expression the past and the future as well as the present. When this is done, the response of the *I Ching* oracle can be truly meaningful in reflecting the wide breadth of time in which a person's life destiny is unfolding.

Having stated the question, I threw the coins. Sitting on a garden chair, Jung bent closely toward the ground and carefully scrutinized the coins as they were settling to the ground. He noted the heads and tails, and made the count. Two points for heads, three points for tails. When the total of the three coins is an even number, it is represented by a broken line. An odd numbered total is represented by a solid line. My first throw yielded two tails and a heads for a total of eight. Thus the first, or bottom, line in my hexagram was a broken line. Jung drew it on a sheet of paper, and motioned to me to throw the coins again.

I threw the coins at Jung's feet while he bent close to the ground and watched them settle. Two heads and a tail gave me seven points for a solid line. He drew this line above the first one. I threw the coins again, and this time all three were heads. I had six points, an even number, for another broken line. Jung examined it carefully and made a knowing expression that was characteristic of him, pursing his mouth and nodding his head, as though to say, "Aha, there is something of special significance to this line." But he did not speak as he did not wish to interrupt the throwing of the coins. Only later did I understand the special significance of that line. Meanwhile he recorded the third line, completing the lower trigram of the *I Ching* hexagram.

I threw the coins for the fourth time and they yielded eight points, two tails and one heads, starting the second trigram with a broken line. The fifth throw produced two heads and one tails for a total of seven, giving a solid line. The sixth and last throw was the same as the fifth for another solid line.

Jung recorded the last throws and handed me the sheet on which my hexagram was recorded. It had a broken line at the bottom, above that a solid line, then two broken lines in the third and fourth places, with two solid lines at the top of the hexagram. Thus the hexagram that resulted from my six throws of Jung's dimes looked like this:

We then discussed the next steps to be taken in my drawing out the meaning, or significance for my life, of the simple act that we had just carried through. How could the act of throwing three coins six times contribute a meaningful awareness of my life? Having formed the hexagram, the next step that Jung indicated for me was that I locate in the text of the *I Ching* the passage that corresponds to that particular hexagram. This would begin the process of correlation by which the *I Ching* is able to speak. By means of these passages within the text, the pattern of lines formed by throwing the coins is related to the question that was posed at the beginning of the exercise.

The *I Ching* way of forming hexagrams by combining solid and broken lines makes possible a total of sixty-four different combinations of lines in sets of six. In the book of the *I Ching*, each hexagram has a text assigned to it. This consists of a basic image, together with various commentaries, elaborations, and judgments pertaining to it. The source of these texts is very ancient, and it is difficult to account for their origin. All attempts to rationalize the method and to isolate a particular theory or intellectual principle as the basis of its operation seem to fail. From a rational point of view within the context of cause-and-effect thinking, there is no discernible reason why the *I Ching* should produce meaningful answers. And yet it does so consistently, even in the case of people who do not "believe" that this is possible.

In his introduction to the English edition, Jung avoided giving a particular theory of what enables the *I Ching* to achieve its results. Instead he carried through an experience of the *I Ching*, asking it the question of what might be expected if it was presented in translation to the modern world. The answer that it brought forth was very meaningful, and opened out in several directions of thought. In refusing to present an intellectual interpretation, Jung was seeking to dramatize the fact that it is not relevant at all to try to show "how" or "why" the *I Ching* operates. Whatever *how* or *why* you may find, no matter how convincing it may seem to be, is not truly the *reason* or the *cause* of it. As Lao Tse says, the way that can be trodden or the way that can be spoken is not the true Tao. Is only appears to be. Wherever you are in your thinking and whatever you understand, the Tao involves a principle that is deeper than that and more elusive. That is very much like saying that the Tao is inherently beyond whatever exists at the present moment, for it includes the *something more than that*. Thus we may move further toward it, but we can never reach it. Jung wished to indicate that this is the very nature of the *I Ching*, that its inner principle consistently moves it *beyond whatever causal condition* is established at any given moment. It is always the *present plus*.

In refusing to give an interpretation of the *I Ching*, Jung was saying two things. The first is that causal analyses are not relevant to the inner principle of the *I Ching*. The second is his inference that the one way in which we may gain entry to a process like that of the *I Ching* is by means of a noncausal principle of interpretation. It was in this connection that he suggested the principle of Synchronicity and developed his hypothesis of it.

To follow the method of the *I Ching*, the next step that Jung indicated to me was that I locate our hexagram in the *I Ching*, consider the images and texts that were assigned to it, and that I explore and extend them as much as seemed valid to me. I returned to my room, and since the *I Ching* was one of the books I had brought to Europe with me, I was able to look it up and work with it immediately while the intensity of throwing the coins with Jung was still fresh. As a result, the entire event, from Jung's first question to the development of the material and my detailed discussion of it with Jung, which covered several days, was experienced by me as a single moment, a single unit of time.

The hexagram turned out to be number 59, *Huan*, the translation being "dispersion," or "dissolution." The upper trigram was designated in the text as *The Gentle* or *wind*; the lower trigram was designated as the abysmal and was identified with water. In Richard Wilhelm's commentary on this combination, he says that wind blowing over water has the effect of dispersing the water and the things that are upon it. In a gentle way it serves to break up blockages.

The text then includes a quatrain that is called *The Judgment*.

> Dispersion. Success.
> The king approaches his temple.
> It furthers one to cross the great waters.
> Perseverance furthers.

Immediately the line, "It furthers one to cross the

great waters," struck me as an uncommonly relevant coincidence. Not that I needed to consult an oracle in order to recognize that my trip over the waters to Europe to work with Jung would have a beneficial effect on my development; but the occurrence of the line in the hexagram that came from my throwing the coins with him was very striking.

The text then continued with a second quatrain given as *the image* of the hexagram.

> The wind drives over the water
> The image of *Dispersion*
> Thus the kings of old sacrificed to the Lord
> And built temples.

After the image is given in the text, there is a section that deals with the individual lines. It does not interpret them individually, but it calls attention to particular lines in terms of their number. In the case of a broken line, the *I Ching* is particularly interested if it is a six. In the case of a solid line, it is particularly interested if it is a nine. The reason for this is that to have a six means that all three coins came as heads. A nine means that all three came as tails. Sixes and nines therefore are complete and perfect. That means also, in the style of *I Ching* thinking, that sixes and nines represent situations that are fully stretched and are extended to their utmost; they are thus the most apt to change. Whatever is fully formed is fulfilled in terms of its potentialities. It is therefore on the verge of changing, perhaps even of going into its opposite.

The *I Ching* thus takes special note of those lines that are formed by coins that are all of one type, the sixes and nines that are either all three heads or all three tails. It makes special provision for them. It uses these lines, which are called *changing lines*, as a means of carrying us to the next moment of time. The *I Ching* procedure enables us to have at least a partial preview of what the situation will be once the line has changed and has brought about a new hexagram. In the text there are individual readings for these *changing lines*.

There was only one such line in my hexagram. The third line was a six. The special reading for that was: "He dissolves his Self. No remorse."

Jung had not given me any specific instructions for working with the *I Ching*, except to indicate that I should see what I could draw from it. His approach in general was to leave things open so that the individual could fill in the spaces that had been left empty. My assumption when I left him that day was that I would use his general method of *amplification*. This is Jung's procedure for working with individual symbols in such a way that the symbol can be extended so that it leads to new awarenesses. All manner of exercises may be used to achieve this, from conscious research on mythological themes, association, and elaboration, to entering the symbol and letting the symbol extend itself from within. This latter technique has been called by Jung *Active Imagination*.

Now, twenty years later, as I read over the records of my *I Ching* experience with Jung, I realize that the elaboration technique was not primarily what I used, but that I followed a procedure that was more reflective of the attitude presented by the *I Ching*. I apparently felt that the *amplification* approach was not applicable in the case of the *I Ching*. Since the imagery was not actually mine but was the imagery of the *I Ching* text, I felt that it was not appropriate for me to extend it.

Jung's method of *amplification* has two fundamental principles behind it. One is the power of the unfolding essence that is contained in deep, transpersonal symbols, the archetypes. This essence opens out much as a seed grows, and it is this that the amplification technique is designed to expedite.

The second principle is that the psyche of each person has its own individuality, and that it can therefore grow only in terms of its own integrity. The corollary of this is that when we practice the method of amplification in order to enlarge our inner symbolic experiences, we can maintain the integrity of the process only when we work with images and symbols that are actually our own in the sense that they have happened within our own inner experience. Otherwise there is an unnecessary dishonesty that breaks the authenticity of the individuation process. It is like a rosebush trying to grow from the roots of a maple tree. There is no need for either to try to grow from the other's roots, since each has its own validity. This is especially true once we understand the organic quality of archetypes that is Jung's great contribution to the study of symbolism.

33

Against this background of thought, I recognized that it would not be appropriate for me to practice *amplification* with the images supplied by the *I Ching*. At the same time, I could not be satisfied to carry out an intellectual elaboration of the *I Ching* text by the light of analytical psychology. That would not have been dynamic enough to express the intensity of the situation. What I did instead was spontaneously use a technique that reflects the inner attitude of the *I Ching*, the technique of *correlation*. This is a technique that has had a much further development in recent years in the context of the Dialogue House Intensive Journal program.

Correlation is a way of working with dreams and images that balances them in relation to the movement of the individual's life, thus establishing a unity of outer and inner in the continuity of life experience. It is a correlation of the life of the person with the movement of his symbols and images. In practice it involves setting side by side the outer and the inner aspects of our lives and letting them speak to one another as each reflects the other. It is a balancing on the one hand of the symbols that occur in dreams and in Twilight Imagery;[1] and on the other hand, either the actual life situation as it is occurring in the present moment, or the pattern of movement that expresses the inner continuity of the life as a whole. We set the two side by side, and we let the correlations

---

[1] See Ira Progoff, *The Symbolic and the Real.* New York: Julian Press, 1963, Chapters 3 and 4. McGraw-Hill paperback, 1973.

between them present themselves to us and speak to us.

The correlation principle is particularly appropriate where the use of the *I Ching* is concerned. In applying it, I noted the words, "dispersion" and "success." Coming at a time when I had written my first book, the main thrust of which was to disseminate Jung's ideas, its relation to my life seemed obvious. To bring about the disperson of ideas seemed to be a main role for me at that time. The oracle's word "success" added encouragement to the very optimistic feelings that were actually present in my life at that time.

The line, "It furthers one to cross the great waters," seemed to correspond exactly and literally to the content of my life. I had just crossed the great waters of the Atlantic to come to Jung. I experienced that line, however, in a further symbolic way. The great waters contain the depth and wisdom of life, and the task that still lay before me was to cross those waters. Thus the *I Ching* was speaking truly to me of my life on two levels simultaneously. It was referring to the literal geographic act that was part of my past and present; and it was pointing in symbolic terms to something that would be a necessary part of my life in the future if my experience in the present was to be fulfilled.

The fourth line, "perseverance furthers," spoke very directly to my feeling of my life at that time. There was inevitably a great exhilaration and excitement as a result of publishing a first book and receiving a fellowship that enabled me to cross the great waters and study with the great man. But the sense was developing within me that the good luck I was enjoying could easily become a danger. It would be necessary for me to get back to work, and to be at least as serious and diligent in the next phase of my work as I had been in the previous one. The phrase "perseverance furthers" therefore spoke directly to the condition of my life, reflecting an awareness that was just below the edge of consciousness. Its sobering effect played an important role shortly afterward in decisions I made concerning the conduct of my work.

I proceeded then to correlate with the situation of my life the second quatrain, *the image*. The lines:

> The wind drives over the water
> The image of dispersion

carried the atmosphere of warning still further, and seemed to me to have more serious overtones than the lines that had gone before. I perceived its correlation to my life to be in terms of the image of the continuous movement of time. It seemed to refer to the breaking up of things that had previously been considered to be solidly established. Now it seemed that the image of the wind as referring to the dissemination of ideas through writing was referring only to the first phase of a cycle. The sense was that, as the wind would continue to blow, it would have a further and opposite effect. The comment I wrote in my

Journal, where I was working with the *I Ching*, w~
"The wind drives things about, breaking apart what
has previously been united."

I continued the process of correlation by interpreting the next two lines in the image. "The kings of
old knew the power of the wind driving over the
water, and they knew that the fact that they were
kings would not protect them from the powers of nature. Therefore they did not exalt themselves, but
were humble and realized that they were only men."
In the words of the oracle, they "sacrificed to the
Lord."

"This is a reminder," I wrote, correlating my reading of the *I Ching* with the inner movement of events
in my life, "that the success spoken of in the first part
of the oracle can be blown away by the wind. The
'kings of old' knew the Tao, so they stayed close to
the earth and worshipped in their temples. They re-
spected the wind on the sea, and they did not exalt
themselves; neither did they attempt to confront the
powers of nature. The fact that they were kings did
not keep them from worshipping."

This line of development in working with the hexagram led me to recall the changing line—the six in
the third place—and the statement that was associated with it. "He dissolves his Self. No remorse."

Now I recognized that the significance of the hexagram in correlation with the movement of my life
was to be found in the changing line. This was the
crucial point at which the events of my life could go

37

in either of opposite directions. My entry regarding the symbolic statement of the oracle reads, "Rather than exalt himself with his success, the king voluntarily foregoes his glory. He does not hold himself high, but considers himself a low and humble being. Thus there is 'no remorse.'" He continues his work with "perseverance" as though there had been no success at all. That is why there is "no remorse."

The changing line in the hexagram represents a delicate point in the life situation, a point of pressure at which a slight movement can precipitate a total change. This is what happens when a small change within the line takes place, when it goes from a six to a seven, and changes from a broken line to a solid line. That small change alters the entire hexagram. With the third line changing, it goes from

It becomes an altogether different hexagram. The correlation of this in the individual's life is that a totally new situation is now depicted. The changing line thus serves as a hinge between the hexagrams. Correspondingly, it serves as the means of connection between two units of time in a person's life. At this point I understood the knowing look of significance that had come over Jung's face when my third throw had yielded three heads.

Continuing to work with the *I Ching* text, my next step was to find in the chart of hexagrams the number of the new hexagram that was formed by the change in the third line. My new hexagram was number 57 entitled *Sun,* the Gentle, the penetrating wind. The two trigrams in this hexagram are identical. The same trigram,

is both above and below. In his commentary, Richard Wilhelm points out that of the sixty-four hexagrams, there are eight that have this symmetry of double trigrams.

In the text accompanying this hexagram, three passages are of importance, the *Judgment,* the *Image,* and the *Sequence.*

The Judgment
The Gentle. Success through what is small.
It furthers one to have somewhere to go.
It furthers one to see the great man.

The Image
Winds following one upon another:
The image of *the gently penetrating.*
In this way the superior man
Spreads his commands abroad
And carries out his undertakings.

The Sequence
The wanderer has nothing that might
receive him; hence there follows the
hexagram of the Gentle, the Penetrating.
The Gentle means going into.

The process of correlation began with the Judgment. The first line, "The gentle. Success through what is small," seemed to speak directly to my life situation at that time. My attention was still very much absorbed by the fact that I had published a book that had become a calling card in establishing a work relationship with Jung. I had, however, felt a psychological ambiguity with respect to that book. On the one hand, as a first book, I was impressed by it; on the other hand, I recognized that in itself it was a small thing to have done. Thus the relevance of the line, "Success through what is small." It helped set things in perspective.

It seemed to me that this line reinforced the comment in the earlier hexagram that "perseverance furthers." As I correlated it with my life, it spoke to a tendency I had observed in myself to turn my attention to large and generalized projects. I interpreted the oracle, therefore, to be cautioning me against that, and to be advising me that the next period in my life should be devoted to carrying out specific studies with painstaking care. In the months that followed this *I Ching* experience, I made the decisions that governed the next decade of my life, and this line from the oracle returned to my mind as a refrain during that time. "Perseverance" and "Success through what is small" became my guideline, counteracting the incautious enthusiasm I might otherwise have followed.

At first I did not know how to establish a relationship to the concept of *the Gentle*, but Wilhelm's commentary clarified it and gave me a lead. Speaking of the hexagram as a whole, he wrote: "*Sun* is one of the eight doubled trigrams. It is the eldest daughter and symbolizes wind or wood. It has for its attribute gentleness which nonetheless penetrates like the wind, or like growing wood with its roots."

Understood in this way, *the Gentle* correlated to my life very meaningfully. Referring to the past, it recalled the feelings of hesitancy and insecurity I had felt at the outset in undertaking my studies of Jung, since that was a time when the university atmosphere was very unfriendly to his point of view. That work had had to proceed very slowly and delicately. For much of the time it was very precarious, and reminded me of Lao Tse's metaphor of a man who walks on tiptoe across thin ice. Everything at that time had to be done very gently and yet it had been successfully completed. I interpreted the oracle to be telling me that I should expect nothing easier in the time to come. What had been true of the past would be true of the future. The oracle was saying that my work would be slow and delicate, but that it could succeed by perseverance in small things.

In that context, the second line, "It furthers one to have somewhere to go," spoke to me clearly. While working in small things, it is very helpful to know the general direction in which one is heading. That was true in the past, and I felt it to be true in the present.

I could not fail to notice also the Synchronicity that was involved in my literally having "some place to go," specifically to Kusnacht-Zurich in Switzerland, where Jung was living.

The next line added to this literal Synchronicity most strikingly. "It furthers one to see the great man." After the first hexagram had given me the line, "It furthers one to cross the great waters," the repeated coincidence of these statements seemed to be too meaningful to be merely chance. But the occurrence of this type of "meaningful coincidence" is one of the phenomena that Jung's hypothesis of Synchronicity is specifically intended to clarify.

The statement about seeing "the great man" may, as is true of most *I Ching* phrases, be read on more than one level. On the literal level, in view of my journey to Switzerland, its reference is obvious. When I read it to him, Jung looked over at me and we smiled at each other in silence. We were acknowledging that the oracle of the *I Ching* was having its little joke. On the second level, however, the statement is symbolic and in the nature of a spiritual teaching.

In working out the correlation between the text and my life situation, I accepted both of these levels of meaning. I took it to be true that I was in fact seeing a "great man," and that this visit would "further" me. I also took it to be true, however, that this literal visit was also a reflection of a symbolic, spiritual level of experience in my life, and that all these aspects were present in the text.

"It furthers one to see the great man," I wrote, "means exactly what it says. The 'great man' in Chinese thought is the man who masters his own spirit. To see such a man does not involve a trip of homage. One is not furthered by seeking prestige or by seeking personal advancement. The way one is furthered when one goes to see the great man is by perceiving and partaking of the special quality of his spirit and his self-knowledge." Thus my trip to Jung seemed to me to be reflected by the *I Ching* on both its literal, external, and its symbolic, spiritual levels.

The specific means by which a person can be inwardly "furthered" when he goes to see a "great man," a spiritual teacher, is difficult. The oracle does, however, give some indication of the way in which it is to be done, for that is the central meaning of the hexagram. *The Image* that follows *The Judgment* in the text describes the way that the great man carries out his life and performs his work.

The key lies in "the image of *the gently penetrating.*" Penetration takes place softly and without pressure. It comes about gradually and is as natural as the process of growth in life. It is like the roots of a tree silently penetrating the earth; or like the wind, following its own nature and thereby encompassing all things. This is expressed in the image of "Winds following one upon another." The task cannot be hurried, but the winds will come as often as they are needed.

At this point I realized that the change of the line in the third place of the hexagram had not only given me a new hexagram but had carried the level of discussion to a logically further point. Given the general question that I had posed at the start of the *I Ching* exercise, the question of my life situation while I was there studying with Jung, the first hexagram enabled me to place myself in relation to the immediate circumstances of my life, my publications, my studies, and especially my attitude toward the work in which I found myself. The changing line, as the hinge between the two hexagrams, carried the situation of my life a step further. It drew it into the future where an additional decision would have to be made and where critical qualities of attitude would be formed. Carried forward by the changing lines, the second hexagram thus anticipated the inner movement of my life. It enabled me to work out a perspective in advance with respect to the priorities in my life and work, and it gave me a basis for working out an approach to the future that was specifically applicable to my individual situation.

Having experienced the relevance of its use and having gained a definite benefit from having worked with the *I Ching*, I was then left with the question of why it should be so. Why should the simple act of throwing some coins in the circumstances of modern times draw forth readings from an ancient text that had a specific personal relevance? That was the question that Jung had also asked, and for which he had attempted to formulate an answer in his concept of Synchronicity.

Two distinct elements are present in the *I Ching* experience. One is the situation at a given moment of time in the life of an individual human being. The other is the act of throwing the coins and relating that by a definite formula to an ancient text. The lines of causality in each of these are quite distinct. They are obviously not causally connected, and yet they have a meaningful relationship to one another. So much so, that in the moment of their meeting, something of extraordinary, significant value is brought about.

Superficially it looks like chance. But to Jung, it was clearly much more than chance, and yet it was not causality either. The specific reasons remained elusive, but to Jung's mind it seemed clear that a principle that has been able to maintain itself over so many centuries in a civilization as sophisticated as the Chinese must contain a secret that is worth discovering. He was convinced that there was a deep and subtle wisdom underlying the *I Ching*, and therefore that the experiences of the *I Ching* constituted an important area to be explored by the modern mind.

IV The Foundations of Synchronicity

Of all his theoretical writings, Jung's efforts to describe and communicate what he means by Synchronicity have met with the least success. This failure is partly due to the elusive and occasionally abstract nature of the concepts. But it is also due in large part to the difficulty of presenting a clear statement of a principle that contravenes the most fundamental habits of modern thinking.

The belief in the primacy of cause and effect is one of the cardinal tenets of the Western view of life. In our time we would surely encounter less opposition in questioning any doctrine of religious faith than in questioning the primary principle of causality. Causality as a belief has been sacrosanct, and yet Jung is far from the first even within the modern scientific era to express doubt as to its total validity. The special contribution that Jung is making now is that through the hypothesis of Synchronicity that he has developed it becomes possible to include causality within the context of a more comprehensive view of the universe.

Two centuries ago, David Hume shook the philosophic world by demonstrating logically that causality is not something we actually see, but that it is only an imputation that we read into events. According to the traditional illustration, one, indeed, that professors of philosophy have overworked on generations of college students, all we actually perceive is one billiard ball touching another with a certain force, and then we see the second ball move away. We do not actually "see" the causality; we only infer it.

By stressing this point, Hume raised some very important questions, but he did not press the matter very far himself; ultimately, in fact, he did little more than hedge and make a polite intellectual retreat. He said that all he wanted to show was that from the epistemological point of view causality cannot be proven as a truth. Certainly, he added, in the daily conduct of affairs it is necessary to believe in causality as though we know it to be a fact, but this gives it no more than a tentative, pragmatic value.

On such a basis, Hume developed the idea that it is because of the necessities of life that causality has emerged as a custom agreed to by everyone and accepted as the practical basis of social activities. He was still thinking of man in rationalistic terms, but since he was an historian as well as a philosopher, the idea suggested itself to him that causality might best be understood as a phenomenon of culture in the context of history.

It was thus in direct continuation of Hume's thought that the American sociologist Thorstein Veblen, who had studied Hume very closely, added his profound analysis to show that the imputations of causality arise as "habits of thought" with historical roots extending deep into specific developments of the past in Western culture. Veblen thus implemented Hume's basic point that causality is not a truth inherent in the things themselves but that it is an imputation that arises pragmatically through social usage.

Beyond that, Veblen went a step further to point out that, quite apart from the question of truth, the historical deep-rootedness of causality as a "social habit of thought" makes it the criterion that all thinking must meet in order to "pass muster" in modern times; and further, that this cultural condition makes it exceedingly difficult for the modern scientist to get outside of causality to examine it critically and to open himself to other points of view. Veblen, like Hume, however, was careful to set a discreet limit to his inquiry and he contented himself merely with describing causality in its various aspects as a pervasive habit of thought that, far from being an absolute category of knowledge, is historically relative in its cultural form.[1]

[1] Thorstein Veblen. *The Place of Science in Modern Civilization*. New York: Viking Press, 1942.

To be able to see causality in so large a perspective involved quite a considerable accomplishment at the first quarter of the century when Veblen wrote. Much has happened since that time, however, to broaden the Western point of view. A primary source of change has been the questioning of causality that has arisen from within the framework of Western science, especially in the work of physicists. In addition to new developments in the philosophy of science, the increasing impact of nonwestern philosophies, particularly the ancient and oriental, has loosened the bonds of causal thought and made it easier to step outside the preconceptions of causality. It is now not difficult at all to conceive that the world may be understood, even better understood, by other principles than causality.

When Jung began to develop the concept of Synchronicity during the nineteen-twenties the increased flexibility of attitudes had not yet emerged. He was greatly stimulated and encouraged by the work of physicists like Nils Bohr and Wolfgang Pauli, but when he published his first systematic version in Germany in 1952,[1] the rigidities of rationalistic causal thinking were still strongly predominant. Since that time, however, the nonrationalist ways of Eastern thinking have greatly enlarged their influence on the Western mind; and the scientists themselves have

[1] C. G. Jung. "Synchronizität als ein Prinzip Akausaler Zusammen-hänge" in C. G. Jung and W. Pauli, *Naturerklärung und Psyche*. Rascher Verlag, Zurich, 1852.

shown an increasing desire to explore new modes of thought.

All in all, there are several factors that have played an important role in the cultural background of Synchronicity. Their effect is not limited to Synchronicity, however, for they are factors that will continue to contribute to the transformation and enlargement of the modern world-view as that change is cumulatively taking place in this generation. The issues and hypotheses that are involved in Synchronicity have an integral place in the process by which a new view of life and the universe is being formed for modern man. For this reason, whether or not Jung's formulation is ultimately accepted, the concept of Synchronicity is bound to play a significant role in the reshaping of the modern mind. It is part of an organic development at profound cultural levels in the history of Western culture.

How can we place the Synchronicity concept succinctly in the perspective of the history of Western thought? In a summary view, it is an outcome of the impact of oriental philosophy on the Western mind once that mind has been opened up by the successive epistemological critiques that stem from David Hume and Immanuel Kant, when it has also considered the implications of recent developments in the physical sciences, and has permitted itself to be inwardly stretched by the nonrational experiences of depth psychology. The total effect of this is to culminate what has progressively been taking place in the history of Western thought. Synchronicity may seem at first sight to be a radical conception that is far from the mainstream of Western thinking. It is actually an outcome of the history of Western thought in which the twofold knowledge of ancient religions and of modern science has been absorbed. For this reason, whether under the name of Synchronicity or not, its contents and orientation are bound to be part of the new directions of thinking in the next decade.

In his early intellectual development, Jung experienced Hume's skepticism and his rationalistic critique of causality through his study of the works of Immanuel Kant. The philosophic traces of this are to be found throughout Jung's psychological theories. It is interesting to note that despite their vastly different backgrounds, Jung and Veblen were drawn in the same general direction as a result of their study of Kant. They both recognized that the categories of knowledge are never absolute, although the "common sense" of every period of history convinces people living within its framework that their particular beliefs about knowledge are fixed and final, universal and eternal. The categories of knowledge, however, no matter how convincingly ultimate they may seem to be at a given time, must be recognized to be historically variable in terms of social circumstances.

Veblen's conception of society was based on an application of Darwinian evolutionism to the study of culture, but Jung derived his historical perspective from the more classically historical work of Jacob Burckhardt. The net result of the two was roughly equivalent. Veblen's approach dissected causality as a Western "habit of thought"; and Jung had the same insight with the conception of the archetypes giving him an additional dimension of psychic depth that was, of course, not available to Veblen.

This is the essential background of Jung's thought when he first began to consider the possibilities of Synchronicity during the late nineteen-twenties. Convinced that causality can no longer be accepted as an absolute reality in itself, but that it must be understood as a psychologically and historically conditioned point of view, Jung turned his attention to cultural approaches that see life in noncausal terms. He wanted to see how the world can be understood if causality is not assumed to be the only possibility.

Seeking to balance the causal point of view, Jung deliberately dealt with all manner of noncausal interpretations, including the mantic or intuitive approach of Astrology, oriental oracles, the Tarot, and other medieval procedures for divining the future. The field here becomes exceedingly broad and difficult to work in because the material is so strange to modern preconceptions that its true meanings are most elusive. The difficulty is only increased by the fact that these noncausal approaches are not considered respectable according to twentieth-century fashions of thought. Even studying them for scientifically valid reasons is suspect, and during the first half of this century Jung suffered considerable ridicule on this account.

Apart from the general philosophical implications of causality, however, Jung felt convinced that it was necessary to have insight into these prescientific procedures if he was to learn how to follow the nonrational workings of the unconscious in his patients. It was therefore in order to meet the needs of his psychological practice as he understood them that he braved the academic scorn—to which, as a matter of fact, he was personally quite sensitive, especially during the early years—and concerned himself with subjects that were in scientific disrepute.

Before he attempted to formulate his conception of Synchronicity in a special study, Jung had been working exploratively with the idea for more than twenty years, observing it empirically in his practice and approaching it from different angles in his seminars. When he finally sat down to write his essay on "Synchronicity as a Principle of Acausal Relationship," he was approaching his seventy-fifth year. He was not yet satisfied with the development he had been able to achieve in his formulations, but he felt that it was essential for him to organize the material and write it down despite the serious handicaps of his illness. He realized full well that much work was still required on both the empirical and conceptual levels, but he felt that his conception of Synchronicity must be articulated at least in some form so that the ideas could be made available for discussion and receive the benefit of suggestions and criticisms from other points of view.

For this reason, as we consider Jung's essay on Synchronicity, we must bear in mind that it was not written as a definitive statement on the subject, but was offered rather as a work in progress. It is consciously incomplete, and even though Jung lived for several years after its publication, it remained so. While this gives the formulations a tentative quality, it also emphasizes the magnitude of the perspective in which the work is conceived and projected. It belongs within a development that involves the enlargement of the scientific point of view in general, as well as an approach to those phenomena that express the psychic nature of man.

The theoretical problems involved in Synchronicity can become quite complicated, but the situations involved are commonly experienced in everyday life. Jung's writings contain many incidents and anecdotes illustrating aspects of Synchronicity, but we may best get a general feeling for the range of problems he was exploring by using a hypothetical example of a very simple kind.

Suppose that you had been concerned about some particular and specialized question and that you had told no one that you were thinking about it. Presently someone comes to see you for reasons that are quite independent and have no relation to your problem. The conversation proceeds according to the purpose of the visit until, quite inadvertently and unexpectedly while not discussing the subject at all, a remark is made that gives you the key you had been looking for.

If we turn to such a situation in retrospect and try to understand the meaning of what happened analytically, it is quite possible for us to follow a chain of causality that will trace each of the events through definite causal links. By cause and effect, we can trace the "reasons" for which you had come to be concerned with that particular problem. Then we can follow analytically how you came to know that particular individual who was visiting you that day, how the appointment for the visit came to be made, and how the lines of the discussion came to develop. All these things could be worked out, and when they were reduced to causal terms they would give the background of the situation as it could be reconstructed from the particular point of view of your life development.

Correspondingly, a similar line of causal analysis could be followed from the point of view of the other person; i.e., the chain of events that caused him to come to visit you; the way he gained the knowledge that turned out really to interest you; how he came to make the appointment with you for just that particular time; how he came "by chance" to make a remark on a subject in which he did not expect you to be interested. All this also could be described in causal terms.

When you and your visitor come together, each of you has a background that stretches back into the past in cause-and-effect terms, and it all comes together at the particular point of your meeting. The arrival of each of you to the point where you are shaking hands and beginning to converse represents the culmination of a vertical line of development moving in a continuous stream out of the past, and operating separately in each of you, each in terms of the pressures and framework of your own experience.

At the moment when you come together, however, all this past causality becomes part of a constellation of the present moment, part of a pattern that goes horizontally across time, and to which the category of causality, which is essentially vertical—that is, continuous in time—cannot apply. Somehow out of this pattern there emerges the additional fact that, inadvertently, you found the answer you had been looking for. Plainly, no causal connection can be demonstrated between the two sets of events, but it is equally plain that *some kind of meaningful relationship* exists between them.

It is perfectly correct to say that it was a coincidence. Then, however, you must add, in order to be clear, that it was a *meaningful* coincidence, inasmuch as the cross linking of events had a definite significance. Since causality in itself does not encompass the fact of coincidence, the most we can say is that cause-and-effect events provide the raw materials with which meaningful coincidences take place. The significance of these coincidences—that is, the special quality of meaning that makes them not simply unrelated events but actual coincidences—is not in any way derived from the background factors that can be traced in terms of causality. They belong to a pattern that is not continuous in time, but that somehow goes across time. For this reason, they involve a principle that, whatever its actual nature, must at least be noncausal.

This essentially simple illustration involves quite a large area of human experience when all its equivalent, related, and derivative aspects are considered. Over the ages, the questions of chance, coincidence, wish fulfillment, cognition through dreams, prayers and their answer, miracles and healings through faith, foreknowledge, and similar phenomena have been explained by various forms of spiritual magic, or have otherwise been dismissed as superstition. Taken by quantity, these experiences constitute a very large percentage of the everyday events taking place not only in so-called primitive or backward societies, but in our modern Western civilization.

In many instances, the history of religion is obviously founded on such events that go beyond causality, but that nonetheless are real. We must recognize, however, that much more than the religious type of phenomena is involved. Even in political history, a field of activity that is ostensibly dependent on rationally guided decisions or at least on diplomatic awareness, we find many crucial events that cannot be causally accounted for. It is certainly for very substantial reasons that the deterministic approaches to history, despite their relevance on the economic level, have to be abandoned as being superficial and woefully inadequate once the larger questions of human destiny are raised.

When we look deeply into the grounds of human activity we find that in all aspects of history, from the subjectivities of religion to the hard facts of politics, from the cold calculations of the business exchange to the intimate relationships of personality, the entire fabric of society is pervaded by events whose meaning eludes the categories of causation. Since the modern rational mind feels compelled to find rigid "laws" to describe the functioning of society and personality, the existence of these unpleasantly nonrational events has had to be ignored.

We must admit that it is exceedingly difficult to interpret them with understanding by any criterion of knowledge; but that is not sufficient reason for ignoring them. Jung, at least, has felt that the importance of the nonrational and the noncausal makes it essential that such phenomena be given the most serious attention. He felt, in addition to the fact that it is not valid to ignore any category of phenomena, that there is some other, more general, principle lying hidden beneath those events. This was the hunch and the spirit of inquiry that lay behind his researches into the Synchronistic phenomena of noncausally related events. It has led to the concept of Synchronicity with its far-reaching implications.

In this connection, we must note the fact that, while Jung's study of Synchronicity began empirically through his being impressed by the frequency of synchronistic phenomena, his reflections on the subject have steadily widened their scope. Ultimately, then, the Synchronistic principle presents itself as a possible way of approach to the general field of scientific study, and also as a guiding principle for various levels of experience of the deep psyche. Synchronicity has become a large affair, at least as difficult in itself as the phenomena it was originally intended to clarify. Before we can consider the value and implications that the Synchronicity conception carries, we must first look at the main historial sources and the way the concept was developed in the course of Jung's work.

V Beyond Causality and Teleology

When Jung began his work as a psychiatrist, he shared the general medical orientation prevalent around the turn of the century. In studying psychosis his aim was necessarily to isolate the "cause." When he developed his famous association tests, the purpose of his work was to devise a diagnostic method by which to find and describe the clusters, or "complexes," of factors that are at the root of abnormal behavior. This medical way of thinking fitted very well with the point of view that Freud was developing.

As Jung began to concentrate on working within the psychoanalytic framework, he did not have to change the basic preconceptions he had absorbed while in medical school. The Freudian concepts merely made it possible to work with the causalistic point of view in a more dynamic way, particularly because of the use Freud made of the concept of energy, or libido. Freud focused the psychiatrist's attention on the instinctual drives in the personality and particularly on the emotional affect that is attached to repressed mental contents. His underlying conception was that the energy present in one form can be converted into energy in another form, specifically that the energy in its converted forms can be used as the motor power for other kinds of behavior. Freud's theory regarding the conversion of repressed sexual contents into artistic creativity in terms of his hypothesis of *sublimation* is an example of this. It involves a general scheme of balancing and conversion of energy forms. In its way, it is a theory of the economics of energy supposing that energy is always transforming itself into equivalent energy forms within the psyche. There is a degree of plausibility in this, but Freud's conception of the psychic conservation of energy made it all too easy to analyze and simplify mental phenomena in terms of cause and effect.

Jung found this conception of energy quite compatible with his own habits of thinking. He eventually articulated it in quite considerable detail in his own conception of analytical psychology. The main change that he felt to be required, however, was that the conception of libido be expanded from Freud's essentially sexual definition to a larger conception of "psychic energy" that would be broader and more comprehensive in scope.

Making this modification, or enlargement, of Freud's view of energy led irresistibly to further changes. Increasingly Jung was impressed by the fact that a dynamic conception of the psyche draws attention to the expansive nature of personality and to the fact that creativity is an inherent quality of the human being. Jung was then led to the recognition that the best way to describe the development of personality is as an unfoldment from within. It is as though a purpose implicit in the nature of the human organism is gradually emerging and maturing out of previous situations in which neither it nor its equivalent was contained. Observing this, he saw that it is seriously misleading to "reduce" the creativity of the "present moment" to the psychic circumstances of the past.

When he wrote the preface for his *Collected Papers on Analytical Psychology*, which appeared in 1920, Jung had already developed far enough along this line of thought to stress the differences between the causal reductionism of Freudian psychoanalysis and the teleological point of view that he was then in process of developing. At that time, however, as Jung still retained much of the earlier point of view, he stated that his psychological interpretations were "not only analytical and causal, but also synthetic and prospective in recognition that the human mind is characterized by *causae* (causes) as well as by *fines* (aims)." He went on to note that "Causality is only one principle and psychology essentially cannot be exhausted by causal methods only."

Teleology thus became the second point of view with which Jung worked. It was clearly an enlargement and improvement on the old reductive procedures, but it was still analytical in nature. It remained essentially rationalistic even while it expanded the knowledge of the nonrational, for it was still direct toward finding the causal nexus of psychic events. At this point in his development, Jung saw clearly the limitations of a causalistic point of view, but he had only begun what was to be a long search for a noncausal perspective.

Teleology does indeed go beyond causality, but it does not leave it behind. The essence of a teleological point of view is the conception of a final purpose implicit in the seed of each organism, with the life of the individual construed as the working out of that purpose. The means by which this implicit aim of life becomes actualized may quite well be described in terms of causal processes; and from the other side, the conception of causality itself may quite acceptably be enlarged to include a teleological point of view.

On close inspection, it appears that teleology and causality do not necessarily contravene one another as general interpretations of the life process. In the actuality of events, it is exceedingly difficult, if not impossible, to mark the point where causality leaves off and teleology begins. It is of the greatest significance, also, to note the fact that while an implicit purpose is contained in the seed of every organism, that purpose is not necessarily actualized and may either develop in a stunted or distorted form or else may not develop at all. The element of contingency becomes of crucial importance, particularly since environmental theories of growth are valid only to a very limited extent. Environmentalism is of little assistance when we come to the larger questions involving the "destiny" of the individual. The very fact that teleology is valid to some degree, the fact that there *is* a purpose inherent in the seed of the individual, and that the dynamic, inner meaning of personal life derives from this purpose place severe limitations on the value of any theory that is oriented toward externals.

Chance appears to play an important role in the working out of the purpose in the seed of individuality. It, however, needs to be a *meaningful* chance, what Jung terms a "meaningful coincidence." The coming together by apparent chance of factors that are not causally linked but that nevertheless show themselves to be meaningfully related is at the very heart of the process by which the purpose of the individual's life unfolds and becomes his "fate." Here teleology and contingency meet. They come together in framing the issue that is the deepest and most difficult to which any study of man can address itself.

Through his practice in psychiatry, Jung came to the question of contingency as a crucial factor in setting the life destiny of the individual. He soon realized, however, that it is not something that can be analyzed in the rational terms of cause and effect. When he turned to study the various "characterologies," the various theoretical efforts to explain individual destiny in terms of some special principle that is worked with either intellectually or intuitively, he observed the limitation that is inherent in all such methods. They are all bound to fail to the degree that they are permitted to become rigid and formal systems, for then they place an artificial stamp on events.

Even astrology, for example, loses whatever ⋁
it might otherwise have when it is interpreted as a
fixed system whose symbols have predetermined
meanings.

In contrast to this, Jung was much impressed by
the insights shown in the ancient Chinese *I Ching*,
"The Book of Changes." When he studied it for
clues, he came to the conclusion that it is altogether
impossible to find the "reason" behind the *I Ching*
intellectually, but that it does work empirically when
it is entered into in the proper spirit. The insights of
the *I Ching* seem to involve a participation in the
flow of events that manages somehow to reflect the
chance factors of time and individuality. This leads
to the inference that, if we are to understand the
aspects of contingency that are expressed in the individual personality, we must first find a means of
bringing our thought into harmony with the movements of life out of which contingency emerges.

In this sense, Jung's development of the Synchronicity principle may be interpreted as an effort to describe a way of thinking—or better, a way of experience—that can comprehend the peculiar pattern of
movement found in nonrational and noncausal phenomena. A key lies in the fact that contingency is
inherently an irrational factor.

Synchronicity thus emerges as the third principle
of interpretation with which Jung has worked. The
three are: Causality, Teleology, and Synchronicity.
In going beyond causality, he developed a teleological point of view for the interpretation of the uncon-

scious; and out of the problems that teleology suggested but could not answer, he was led to Synchronicity. All three have remained in Jung's thought, applied according to the problem and situation. The teleological point of view retains the pivotal position in his thinking because it contains cause and effect within it and yet it leads directly into the issues of Synchronicity. Synchronicity, however, is an independent principle, balancing and complementing the others.

VI Leibniz and Tao

Although it is not primarily an intellectual concept, Synchronicity has had formidable philosophical exponents in the past. In relating Jung to Hume and Kant, as we have done, the point was to indicate the historical process by which Jung's thinking emerged from the rationalism of modern Western philosophy. The main philosophical antecedents of Synchronicity in Western culture, however, are to be found in sources far beyond rationality. They are typified by Leibniz as its leading representative in modern times.

Leibniz's *Monadology* culminates the rich development of European alchemical thought and epitomizes the conception of man as a microcosmic expression of the macrocosm. This symbolic conception is found in a variety of forms in the ancient and oriental worlds, and it flourished again at the close of the Middle Ages in Europe in those philosophies that went beyond the bounds of orthodox thought.

Ostensibly, Leibniz developed his conception of the monad, i.e., the microcosm, in the form of a rationalist philosophy in keeping with the mood of the seventeenth century. The full intention of his work, however, can be comprehended much more fundamentally as a way of experiencing the world. This larger goal of Leibniz's work was more clearly brought out in a work other than the *Monadology,* namely, his *Principles of Nature & Grace.* Here we see the purpose of personal application that underlay his work.

Leibniz's basic conception of the cosmos postulates a "pre-established harmony" designed and maintained by God. In practice, however, God does not intervene. The meaning of the "pre-established harmony" is thus that the universe is to be understood as a vast pattern in which all the individual parts, the monads, are interrelated. All of the monadic entities in the cosmos have their inherent characteristics according to their nature, and according to their place within the pattern of the universe. In addition, they contain an image of the pattern of the universe within themselves.

Each monad is closed off separate from all the others, as though it were hermetically sealed; for, as Leibniz says, "the monads have no windows through which anything may come in or go out."[1] On the other hand, the monads reflect the larger pattern in themselves, so that each monad is "a perpetual living mirror of the universe."[2] Human beings, as monads, participate in the moving patterns of the cosmos and

[1] Leibniz, *The Monadology,* #7.
[2] Ibid, #56.

reflect them. Leibniz says, "Every body responds to all that happens in the universe, so that he who saw all could read in each one what is happening everywhere, and even what has happened and what will happen."[1]

The individual monads themselves are sensitive to the workings of the universe and of the other monads, but this sensitivity varies according to the nature of the monad. While the fact that the microcosm reflects all the world results in a perception *of* all things *by* all things, this perception is largely unconscious. Only in small proportion does it become "apperception," which is Leibniz's term for that part of perception that reaches the level of consciousness. The reason for this limitation is that "a soul can read in itself only what is represented there distinctly. It cannot all at once open up all its folds, because they extend to infinity."[2]

The knowledge that comes to the individual monad unconsciously Leibniz refers to as the "small perceptions." They are always present latently in the soul, but they become manifest in a variety of forms as the individual monad matures toward "perfectibility" and expands its relation with the universe. This basic conception is quite in accord with the view of the Self that Jung has developed so that, looked at from one point of view, we can say that Jung's psychology now begins to make possible the empirical documentation

[1] Ibid., #61.
[2] Ibid., #61.

and modern practice of Leibniz's monadological view of man and the universe.[1]

One of the most significant aspects of Leibniz's work as far as Synchronicity is concerned is his formulation of the relation between the body and the soul. Academically his theory has been classified as "psychophysical parallelism" and has been thinned down to the point where it has become philosophically a white elephant in modern thought. Now, however, with the formulation of the Synchronicity principle and with the work done by Jung in observing the depth phenomena of the psyche, we can begin to see some of the hidden implications of Leibniz's conception. Indeed, it opens numerous possibilities for modern thinking, especially with respect to those obscure issues that arise at the point of relationship between the inner cosmos of the human psyche, and the other cosmos of the universe as a whole.

One of the senses in which Leibniz speaks of the monad is as the seed of potentiality, the inherent living essence of the organism. It is quite the same thing as Jung's referring to the Self as the all-encompassing archetype of the human person.[2] In this sense Leibniz uses the term "monad" as equivalent of "soul" in its most general meaning. Body and soul draw themselves to each other, correspond to each other, and have a lasting affinity for each other because of the way in

[1] Progoff. *The Death and Rebirth of Psychology,* Ch. VI, "C. G. Jung at the Outposts of Psychology." New York: Julian Press, 1956. McGraw-Hill paperback, 1973.
[2] Ibid., p. 177, "The Self as Symbol and Reality."

which the universe has been established. It is simply in the nature of things, or, as Leibniz would put it, it is inherent in the "pre-established harmony."

The body is the specific point at which the infinite possibilities of knowledge in the monad are crystallized, are brought together, and inherently, are also given limitation. "Although each created monad represents the whole universe," Leibniz says, "it represents more distinctly the body which specially pertains to it and of which it constitutes the entelechy. And as this body expresses all the universe through the interconnection of all matter in the plenum, the soul also represents the whole universe in representing the body, which belongs to it in a particular way."[1]

Body and soul are separate, and they operate by independent principles. Nonetheless, they also go together, for "they are fitted to each other in virtue of the pre-established harmony between all substances, since they are all representations of one and the same universe."[2]

Even while they are so closely linked, body and soul function in terms of different laws. "Bodies act," Leibniz says, "in accordance with the laws of efficient causes"—and this means that we are to interpret the physical world as being determined by the principles of cause and effect. On the other hand, "Souls act in accordance with the laws of final causes through their desires, ends and means."[3] The soul, in other words,

1 Leibniz. *The Monadology,* #62.
2 Ibid., #78.
3 Ibid., #79.

71

contains a purpose in its nature, and its life consists in the working out of this purpose. The soul is therefore teleological in its operation while the body follows causality.

These dichotomies seem to be rather overdrawn when looked at from the modern point of view. Physics no longer permits us to consign all the physical world to a strict causality, and teleology tells only part of the story of the soul, or psyche. Yet, the essence of what Leibniz said goes right to the heart of the modern problem. Wherever it is still contained within a medical point of view, Depth Psychology treats the soul as though it were part of the physical world subject to the principles of a rigid causality. When Jung realized the inadequacy of causality as a principle of psychological interpretation, he turned to a teleological point of view similar to that which Leibniz had described as the operating principle of the soul. In contrast to the original position of Freud, we now find an increasing tendency toward Holistic theories that interpret the psyche from different conceptual approaches in terms of its purposiveness.[1]

We have already indicated, however, that the principle of teleology is also limited, so that when we follow it to its full implications it leads us to a point where we must realize that something more is necessary. This is the process of thought that led Jung to begin to work with Synchronicity. A commensurate

[1] See in this regard, Progoff, *Depth Psychology and Modern Man*. New York: Julian Press, 1959, Chapters 6 and 7. McGraw-Hill paperback, 1973.

insight is involved in Leibniz's formulation of the functioning of body and soul. Leibniz considers both causality and teleology as partial principles whose operation is possible only because of the larger context that sustains them. "The two realms," Leibniz says, "are in harmony, each with the other."[1]

At this point, an interesting correlation emerges, and it has the greatest significance for the hypothesis of Synchronicity. The body follows the principle of causality; the soul follows the principle of teleology; but the larger context, which contains them in harmony, cannot function by either of these principles. Body and soul subsist together as parts of a pattern that is the universe as a whole. The significance of the "pre-established harmony" is that it sets the pattern within which the diversities of life may have their "interconnections."

The principle by which the "pre-established harmony" operates can be described as a maintenance of relationship between things that are bound to each other neither by any definite causal nexus, nor by the inner "entelechy" of the monad. It involves a holding together of the pattern of things, and this means that the individual and separate entities must be maintained in correspondence to each other as part of the harmonious pattern of the cosmos. The harmony of this pattern is not to be explained. It is simply the way the universe is. It is simply how the cosmos has been "pre-established" to provide the con-

[1] Leibniz, *The Monadology*, #79.

73

ditions for life. It is what Jung has referred to, borrowing a phrase from Kipling, as "Just so!" And it is what the ancient Chinese referred to as "Tao," the primary ground of Being, the pervading principle of patterning and meaning in the cosmos. The principle by which the patterns of life are held together is neither causation nor teleology, but a principle that binds the entities of body and soul together.

The master principle of the cosmos is thus not something that can be analyzed or measured. It is a subtle, hidden principle of correspondence that is somehow inherent in the patterning of the world. It is a principle that has had a fuller development in the East than in the West, but by the time Leibniz used it, it already had a substantial European history. Jung has drawn upon this history for the contents of his concept, and stressing the patterning of each particular moment of time, he has given it the name "Synchronicity."

The work of Leibniz provides the best background for understanding the perspective that Jung is trying to build, especially with reference to the development of Western thought. In general it is correct to say, however, that Leibniz came to the principle of correspondence with a rational orientation particularly with the aim of comprehending it and mastering it as a principle of nature. Only one aspect of the point of view with which Jung approaches Synchronicity is contained in this. Quite another aspect is articulated in the ancient philosophy of Tao.

Since Taoism follows an essentially similar conception of the cosmos, it is quite legitimate for Jung to claim that both Leibniz and Lao Tse are forerunners and sources of his conception of Synchronicity. There is also, however, a significant difference between the two, a difference that extends quite deeply into the traditional development of Western thought. Leibniz seeks to grasp the pattern of these elusive relationships and intangible influences in order to hold it firmly in his mind. Tao, however, does not seek to grasp it, but to become part of it, to enter into the movement of the patternings of time that comprise the harmonious flow of nature.

We have already seen that the conception of the world as "Tao" corresponds to Leibniz's "pre-established harmony," but Leibniz, in characteristically Western fashion, set "God the architect"[1] over it to design it and to keep it in proper order. The Eastern point of view does not admit any outside agency. Tao is quite enough, since it is everything. The way that Tao follows is to participate in the harmony of nature in order to have the living experience of being at one with the world. There is the equivalent of this in Leibniz, as anyone who reads him with understanding will realize, but it is orientated to meet the requirements of a European man of the world. Tao is attuned in a more interior way, and that is perhaps more suitable for bringing us close to the subtle medium in which Synchronicity operates. Jung quotes Chuang Tse as saying, "If you have insight, you use

[1] Leibniz. *The Monadology,* #89.

your inner eye, your inner ear to pierce to the heart of things, and have no need of intellectual knowledge." And Jung comments, "This is obviously an allusion to the absolute knowledge of the unconscious, or the presence in the microcosm of macrocosmic events."[1]

---

[1] C. G. Jung. *Synchronicity: An Acausal Connecting Principle,* p. 489, in Jung, *Collected Works,* Vol. VIII, Princeton, N.J.: Princeton University Press, 1960.

VII Archetypes and the Patterning of Time

If we now consider the details and implications of what Jung has in mind when he speaks of the "knowledge of the unconscious," we shall be able to see the psychological foundations on which his approach to Synchronicity rests, and the way it emerges from his larger experience of the world.

One of the important methods that Jung developed in his therapeutic work as an effort to draw his patients along the road to "wholeness" was a technique called "Active Imagination." The name of this is misleading because a loosening of the imagination as in free association is by no means what it involves. It calls, rather, for an intense attentiveness to the larger and more significant figures and symbols that arise out of the deeper layers of the unconscious in dreams and fantasies. Underlying the development of this method was Jung's conception that the psyche carries all the necessary answers within itself. He was not thinking in terms of consciousness, however. In fact, his conception was quite the opposite of the conscious introspection that looks into the personality for self-analysis.

The principle behind "Active Imagination" is to encourage or stimulate the psyche in such a way that it will express what is latent in it. It seeks to work on the symbolic level to draw forth the instinctual, generic drives and also those deeper generic images by which the human personality, as a part of nature, reflects the macrocosm in the unfulfilled seed of its being. It is because of the application of this conception of personality as a universe in miniature that Jung's psychological methods inherently go beyond psychology.

In the framework of Jung's microcosmic/macrocosmic conception of the human psyche, to work with the materials of personality, which means to work *within* the human being, leads immediately beyond the person. This is so because, at its depth, the psyche of the individual contains *reflections* of the larger universe. These reflections are images symbolically representing aspects of the macrocosm. The images contained within the individual psyche are thus reflections of the universe in miniature. The movements of these within each person embody the processes of the psyche. They are the expressions in individual form of the processes and rhythms that move in the macrocosm of nature. In this context we can see how it is that Jung's psychological perspective makes it possible to give an empirical demonstration in experience of the view held by Chuang Tse that the "inner eye" does not need intellectual knowledge because it comes into harmony with the cosmos when it looks into itself.

At such a point of meeting, the relation between Jung's depth psychology and the subtle depth philosophy of Taoism becomes explicit. For Jung, however, it does not remain merely a point of view, or *Weltanschauung*. His effort is to work it out empirically by determining the specific forms in which the macrocosm becomes manifest in the microcosm of human personality. This is the purpose of his analysis of archetypes, and it is the real foundation of his theory of Synchronicity.

Putting the discussion back in terms of Leibniz for the moment, we note that the conception of the psyche as microcosm corresponds to the monad. For Leibniz, the monad represents the essence of the human being, containing as it does the fullest potentiality of the person and implicitly the striving toward "perfectibility," which is the principle underlying life activity. While the monad contains both body and soul within it, each independent and yet in a close relationship with the other, the creative and therefore decisive factor is the soul. The correlations of this with Jung's thinking are very important, especially with respect to his larger view of the Self as expressing the encompassing wholeness of the human person.

In Jung's view of the Self as corresponding to the monad, the Self contains the basic nature of the species, and most especially its life principle manifests dynamically by means of its psychic expressions. The Self, however, is not to be comprehended only as the seed containing the purpose latent in the personality. It is also, as a small part of the universe containing the essence of the universe in miniature, a direct point of contact with all the world. The Self therefore contains the empirical realities of personality, and it is also a *substrate of reality* in the largest sense of the term. It is the link with the universe, and when it is experienced in this way, it becomes a kind of continuum on a psychic level. This is the level on which the Self corresponds both psychologically and cosmically to Tao and to Leibniz's "Universal Harmony," which is, after all, merely the macrocosmic aspect of the monad.

In the more limited sense of the self as a reality that is empirically experienced, Jung speaks of the *psychoid* aspect of personality. This refers to the level at which the psyche has not yet achieved a distinctly psychological quality. It is somewhat similar to what finally develops as psychological activity, but the necessary processes of differentiation have not yet taken place.

In describing the patterns of behavior found in all species of the animal kingdom and the quasi-psychological foreimages that go with them, Jung deals with a level of life that is immediately close to nature. All future possibilities are fused together in the psychoid state, for it is a level of existence that is not yet sufficiently advanced for separation and distinctness to be necessary. The psychoid state is thus very much like the Self conceived as cosmos or as a primal chaos. It would in fact be correct to say that the psychoid level of development corresponds in the microcosm to the primal chaos in the universe.

Proceeding on this basis, the aim of Jung's analysis of archetypes and instinct is to provide a substantial empirical foundation on which to understand the differentiation that eventually takes place in the development of personality. The archetypes are a next step in the unfoldment of the foreimage that is attached to the instinct just before it reaches the point where its characteristics become distinct. The archetypes and the instincts then emerge from the same root and yet are opposites engaged in a more or less constant tension with one another. From this tension, the energy at the disposal of the psyche is generated, or, it would be better to say, through this natural tension the energy latent in the organism is given a peculiarly psychic character.

This is one way to look at it. From this direction we get what may be called a "worm's-eye view" of human development regarded from the point of view of how man emerges from nature. Jung feels that it is quite essential to look at the psyche from this perspective, but that it is equally essential to realize that this is only one point of view from which the psyche can be seen. Within the terms of the evolution of the animal kingdom, the basis psychological images arise from the patterns of behavior that are native to the human species, drawing both their symbolic tendencies and the great motor power of their energy from primal sources deep in nature.

From the other point of view—the "bird's-eye view"

—the human organism is seen as a minute representation of the cosmos. The basic patterns of behavior are then conceived as mirrorings of the macrocosm in the microcosm. The Self of the individual, which means the totality of the person, is then a reflection of the cosmos as a whole. Jung refers to this under a great variety of terms and wishes mainly to stress that we are here dealing with a fundamental and universal fact that has been perceived and recorded under a great many symbols and concepts including the psyche, Self, the unconscious, and Mercurius, not to mention the many specialized and esoteric symbolisms throughout mankind. The essential qualities of these, however, are the same as what is contained in the more empirical conception of the primary psychoid state of the human being; namely, that the body and mind, the biological and the psychological, have not yet been differentiated, and the instincts and archetypes are still fused together, neither having yet emerged with their characteristic qualities. The patterns that arise within the processes of evolution as the psychoid, nonpsychic ground of human development, are thus correspondences of the universe manifested in the individual being.

In this same context, just as the process of psychic emergence as a whole is a microcosmic correspondence of the macrocosm, the archetypes can be spoken of as being "psychological" only in a proximate sense, for they likewise are mirrorings of the cosmos. Our empirical justification for such a statement is mainly the intimations and overtones that archetypal symbols carry with them. As representations of the underlying processes of life and death and rebirth, of the struggle of opposites and their resolution, archetypal images in their multitude of social and historical forms draw human beings into connection with the primary, most pervasive processes of the universe.

The experience of an archetypal symbol results in a sense of relationship to the interior workings of life, a sense of participation in the movements of the cosmos. The individual at such moments feels his individuality to be exalted, as though he were transported for an instant to a higher dimension of being. Clearly, the situation that is established when an archetype becomes active in human life is more than personal. It is felt to have what Jung speaks of as a *"cosmic character,"* and this derives from the fact, as he says, that it appears in the individual as a "complementary equivalent of the 'outside world.' "[1] It is experienced with a great intensity, accompanied by a great emotional affect, and it brings an awareness of a special light, a numinosity carrying a sense of transcendent validity, authenticity, and essential divinity.

An extraordinarily great concentration of energy seems to be at work in this. The energy that is involved in it must be understood in a double sense. On the one hand it derives from the transcendent aspect of the archetype as a manifestation of the macrocosm in microcosmic form; on the other hand, it expresses a natural fact, that great intensities of energy are acti-

[1] C. G. Jung. *Aion,* p. 196 *in Collected Works,* Vol. IX, Part II.

vated when the human being touches the psychoid level of his nature where instinct and archetype are fused as one. The transcendent and the natural go together through all creation bound by a mutual inner connection. On the one hand, "divinity" is latent in matter and requires material forms; on the other hand, no individual entity could live if there were no spark of macrocosmic reality in its seed.

In understanding what is involved in the individual's experience of archetypes, we must realize that while the experience takes place as a psychological phenomenon, it is as a phenomenon that is by its very nature more than psychological. Its primary force comes from the fact that it has a spiritual quality and that it validates itself existentially in a person's life. The manifestation of the macrocosm in the microcosm means that something of the world's divinity has been individualized. When a personality experiences this and participates in it, the experience serves as a link between the human being and God. Since this is so, the sense of numinosity and the intimations of spiritual transcendence that go with it are essentially correct.

At such times, nonetheless, it is exceedingly important to distinguish between God and the *image of God* that is actually being experienced by the individual as a psychological event within his personality.[1] The fact of experiencing a relationship with God

[1] Ibid., p. 195.

must be understood as a psychological event because it necessarily takes place within a human psyche. The psyche is, however, only the place, as it is the focus, of the manifestation; the event itself is more than psychological since it involves the drawing up or activation of a reflection of God that has been latent in the individual.

The relationship that then results from the awareness of God as experienced within the personality is best described as a *situation of correspondence.* This correspondence is between the microcosm and the macrocosm, for a harmony has been achieved and the individual has come into an equivalent union with the universal. Such correspondences are implicit in the nature of life, but they are latent. Only when they are activated and brought to realization does their great *wirkende Kraft,* the vital power that is inherent in the archetypes as correspondences of the cosmos, become effective.

When an archetype is experienced in this fundamental aspect, a new situation is created. A new pattern is constellated. The phenomena that then come into the human range of knowledge tend to give the impression that a great new force of energy has been let loose in the world. This is apparently so, but it is not the essence of those situations in which the numinosity inherent in the archetypes has been actualized as a correspondence of the macrocosm. It is undoubtedly because of this energic aspect that the events that express such correspondences in time are generally referred to by symbols that are the equivalent of energy —as Divine Power, Mana, Magnetic Force, spiritual potency, and so on.

Symbols of this type provide the basis and the essential principle behind the primitive imputation of miraculous effects, or what Jung calls "magic causality." Energy is, however, not the primary factor involved. It is rather that when the correspondence between the macrocosm and microcosm takes place, a new pattern is set up in time, and this has a reshuffling effect on the entire environment pertaining to the event. It changes the configuration of the situation that had previously been in existence. As the new pattern is formed, other situations and events outside of it are drawn into relation to it in a new way. There then takes place a regrouping and a restructuring of its internal and external elements, reconstellating all the factors in relation to one another. The result is a new, ever-enlarging crystallization of patterns.

A great power certainly seems to be at work in such cases, but it is not to be described in terms of energy. Energy is certainly involved in what takes place, but the constellation of situations depends mainly on a restructuring that determines the patterns from within. If we are to speak in terms of energy, then, it would have to be something other than energy that is capable of being mechanistically determined in terms of cause and effect.

The principle at work is apparently an interior one, although something in its nature enables it to extend across time and space. It does not directly change events or conditions in themselves, but it brings a *reordering* of the pattern of things within which specific situations and conditions are contained. Contexts and meanings thus change imperceptibly. Since a factor of change is involved, we may say that there is a "power" at work, and that this should be characterized as a form of energy. We may suppose further that this energy would be capable of causal analysis if it were only not so subtle and intangible as to prevent us from laying our hands on it and dissecting it.

On closer look, however, we see that it would not be correct for us to speak of this "power" as energy, for we would then be postulating it as a definite factor, as an entity that is itself involved in the situation. When a pattern is set up in time by the activation of an archetype, however, the crucial factor does not seem to be an external agency of any kind but rather an *ordering principle* that is inherent in the fact that a pattern is being formed. What holds the pattern together, then, is not vectors of energy but an *interior cohesion,* some principle of *interior binding* (a principle of holding together) that operates within and across the prevailing pattern, maintaining the pattern as a whole in terms of the interior correspondence of its constituent parts.

We seem then to be confronted with a situation that involves something akin to correspondence in its traditional sense of a drawing-to or attraction of opposites within the context of a basic sameness. The simplest and probably most graphic example of this, if we understand it symbolically, is the attraction of the opposite sexes within a given species. Always, whether they be human beings, monkeys, or reindeer, the sexes are contained by the common unity of their species. Within this unity, however, as male and female, they are opposites of each other. More significantly, while they are opposites within a single species, each contains something of its opposite in its nature.

The best conceptual representation of this is the ancient Yang/Yin sign of Tao.

In that representation, the opposites of Yang and Yin are brought together to comprise a unifying whole, and each significantly contains a small part of its opposite within itself. It is indeed relevant with reference to the simple example of the sexes that modern research has validated the intuitive, essentially symbolic, insight of the ancient Taoist by uncovering the "biological" foundation for the fact that each sex does contain something of its opposite in its nature. Tao thus expresses a cosmic principle in a highly concrete form. Sexual opposites, like every set of polarities that can be represented by the Yang/Yin sign, are manifestations in the microcosm of the macrocosmic principle of opposites. The universe reflects itself in all its parts, and that is why every separate entity is a symbol of the pattern of the universe as a whole. It is the principle of outer correspondence that holds the parts together, thus maintaining the patterns of time; and equally, it is their interior correspondence that maintains the relationship by which the microcosm expresses the aspect of the macrocosm that is present in it.

The archetypes that are present in the psyche derive their great power from the fact that what they express in the human beings is more than human in nature. Their correspondence to aspects of the *interior orderedness* provides the basis for a patterning across time that is enforced not by energic causation but by an inner consistency of qualities. As the archetype is experienced in the individual personality, the question of whether it is numinous, that is, whether it generates an inspiring and energizing power in the psyche and casts an unusual light or atmosphere around itself, depends on the depth at which it is contacted. A complex of psychic factors basically archetypal in nature may be experienced superficially by an individual, and then the force potential in it will dwindle away before it has been truly formed. On the other hand, if the archetype is entered into deeply and its full potentiality is drawn forth and actualized, the result is a numinosity of highest intensity so that the archetype then becomes much more than a psychological image. It becomes a "living power," a center around which new patterns of events constellate in time.

The degree to which the macrocosm is reflected in the microcosm has two main aspects. The first involves the depth to which the experience of the archetype penetrates; the second involves the state of the psyche as a whole, particularly the condition and environment in which the archetype finds itself when it becomes a living factor for the personality. On this depends the intensity and the clarity, and ultimately also the validity and the consequences, of the experience taking place. The most basic point in understanding what is involved here is the fact that the archetypes cannot be contained within the ego-centered consciousness.

In the context of Jung's thought, both the ego and consciousness as a whole must be understood as being themselves unconscious in their origin and in their essential mode of operation. Consciousness arises from the psychoid foundations of personality, and always depends on patterns of behavior and psychic contents that are primarily unconscious. The expression of the archetypes as autonomous manifestations of the deeper layers of the psyche necessarily takes place beyond the ego and consciousness. Everything depends therefore on the condition and form in which the archetypes are expressed, and especially their relation to the contents of the rest of the psyche. Most essentially, the archetypes exert themselves *upon* the ego and upon consciousness. When they work together with them, they do so by drawing the ego and consciousness into the orbit of an archetypal constellation. The optimum relationship that can then result in the ideal case is an harmonious complementation, a reciprocal balancing, in which the archetypes supply the basic psychic contents and set the direction while the ego and consciousness channelize, clarify, and guide the process as a whole to assist in actualizing the aims that the psyche unconsciously contains.

The condition in which the psyche is internally balanced by an integration of consciousness and the unconscious in mutually supporting roles is the most creative state to which the psyche can be brought. As this integration encompasses the psyche in its largest aspect, drawing the personal factors of the psyche into macrocosmic connections, this unity involves the Self as a whole in its double aspect as the primary ground of psychic realities and also as the reflector of the cosmos in man.

The Self is the archetype of all the archetypes that the psyche contains, for it comprehends within itself the quintessential purpose behind both the impersonal archetypes and the archetypal process by which the ego and consciousness emerge. The Self may be understood as the essence and aim and the living process by which the psyche lives out its inner nature. As such the Self can never be contained by the ego or by any of the specific archetypes. Rather, it contains them in a way that is not limited by space or time. The way the Self contains the various contents of the psyche is in a kind of "atmosphere," a state that is more than psychological, an "aura" that sets up the feeling of the situation in a manner that is neither psychological, nor spatial, nor temporal. It involves something that can best be spoken of as a nonphysical continuum by means of which the correspondences within the cosmos, the microcosm and the macrocosm, come together to form patterns, at once transcendent and immanent, and constellating situations that draw physical as well as psychological phenomena into their field.

The patterns of events that then emerge appear as "confluences" that spread the framework of their pattern across a given moment of time. These events are often quite dissimilar in their outward appearance as well as in their causal origins. and their significance as parts of the common pattern is thus easily missed. Within the pattern of the moment, however, these events always correspond to each other in some meaningful way, and in order to understand them it is necessary to perceive the essential meaningfulness of their relationship, which involves the *interior orderedness* within the pattern of correspondences. When this is comprehended, events that cannot otherwise be understood in terms of their causal connections reveal their nature as *synchronistic phenomena,* that is, as individual parts of a pattern constellated across time and centered around an archetypal factor that draws other factors of all kinds into its "atmosphere."[1]

---

[1] Ibid., p. 167, 168.

VIII The Synchronistic Ground of Parapsychic Events

We can now understand more fully what Jung had in mind when he refered to the unconscious capacity of knowledge present in the psyche. It is inherent in every process of nature, including the psyche, that the seed of each process contains an implicit foreknowledge of the goal toward which it is unfolding. This is a quality of knowledge that expresses itself on nonconscious levels. It is experienced as an intimation of things to come. Particularly in the human experience of it, this quality of the organic teleology of the life process reflects itself in intuitions that seem to come just a little bit ahead of time in relation to the actual outcropping of events.

It is interesting to note in this regard that when Jung described what he called the "intuitive type," the major characteristic he assigned to such persons is that their interests are almost compulsively drawn toward the future and the planning of future activities. It may be that what Jung was perceiving and describing there was the "psychological type," or better, the psychological situation, which may arise in the life of any type of person, by which an individual becomes sensitive to the next emergent phase of his life process. The reason that the organic teleology of the life process can be experienced by sensitized individuals in this way is that the entire process that is due to unfold is present in the seed of the person where it can be inwardly perceived in nonconscious ways. The goal or purpose of the events to follow is present as an image in the psyche at the time that the process is set in motion and begins to unfold.

The type of unconscious knowledge that is involved in this is relatively easy to understand. It is most frequently revealed in dreams or psychic phenomena of an equivalent nature. There is, however, another type of unconscious knowledge that is more difficult to understand. This is the kind that is not restricted to future developments within the psychic and physical organism of the individual, but involves the direct knowledge of events separated either by space or time, or both, while they are not connected by any tangible medium of communication. Included in this is the major area of what has been called "Extrasensory Perception," or "ESP," the study of which has become the main subject matter of the rapidly growing field of Parapsychology.

Jung's approach to these phenomena rests on his conception of the Synchronicity of events as an aspect of the patterns existing across each moment of time. We have already discussed the main basis for this view, deriving as it does from ancient doctrines whose leading exponent in the modern Western tradition is the great Leibniz. The central and all-encompassing conception is that each individual unit of creation is a miniature reflection of the cosmos.

Leibniz himself spoke of the "small perceptions" of the monad as the means by which the reflection of the outer world takes place. These perceptions are always unconscious, and they do not ordinarily reach consciousness unless the normal condition of the psyche has been altered in some way. Very often, such "subliminal" perceptions simply "pop" into consciousness through an uprush or temporary "possession" by what Jung calls a "complex," a cluster of unconscious contents; or they may come into consciousness through a break in the psychic fence whose function it is to keep unconscious perceptions out of range of the ego. The most fundamental way in which they may become available to consciousness, however, is when a restructuring occurs in which a new condition is established in the psyche as a whole.

If consciousness is then brought into close relation to the unconscious in such a way that it becomes sensitive to the level of the psyche at which the world is reflected in the individual, the unconscious capacity for knowledge becomes a major component of personality. In such a condition of integration, the essential quality of the Self becomes real. The Self can then be experienced as the pervading ground of personality, as the psyche reaches beyond itself to the world and becomes the medium by which the macrocosm is made manifest in the microcosm.

This is the more general aspect of the way in which knowledge comes to man directly via his unconscious capacities. It assumes a special importance, however, when it is particularized so as to make the perception of specific situations and events possible. Here we discover the practical consequences of the conception of *patternings across time* whose individual parts reflect each other in a way that is not conditioned by space relationships. The ground via which these "reflections" are transmitted is the *Self,* conceived as both the fundamental reality of personality and as the continuum connecting man and cosmos. It is in these terms that Jung looks to the phenomena of the Self as they take place within the *patternings across time* to find clues to the nature of that part of cognition that is experienced via the unconscious.

In studying the phenomena that are now becoming the special province of Parapsychology, the perception of events at a distance or the previsioning of future happenings, Jung takes it as self-evident that such events do actually occur. Their occurrence is their proof, and for Jung, the most convincing evidence is the numerous occasions on which he experienced them in his psychiatric practice and in his personal life. Events of a parapsychic type are bound to occur for anyone who is living in close connection with his unconscious, whether that connection is expressed through either of its opposite forms, through the conscious development of larger cognitive capacities in a sensitive personality, or through an uncontrolled predominance of the unconscious, as in psychosis.

Jung therefore begins by taking for granted as fact the validity of the class of phenomena whose existence parapsychologists have sought to prove by their laboratory studies. These laboratory studies have resulted in impressive statistics that end by confirming the opinion formed on the basis of sensitive observation. They support Jung's original view that these phenomena occur so often that their existence is an obvious fact, and that the pressing need is not to continue to prove their existence but rather to find some means of understanding them. Jung's principle of Synchronicity thus comes in at a point further along the road of Parapsychology. He takes the events for granted, and attempts to formulate a working hypothesis that can serve as a basis for integrating and interpreting the data.

Rhine's researches were of interest to Jung in certain significant respects. Their main importance to him arose from the fact that Rhine's studies indicated that something more than causality is involved in parapsychic phenomena. In saying this, however, we must realize that Rhine himself was by no means inclined to put such an interpretation on his work. He was content to observe that the statistical results of his experiments in card guessing, or in guessing the throw of dice, went beyond the limits of probability. In Rhine's view, the significance of this lay in the fact that it demonstrated that parapsychic phenomena cannot be explained away as mere chance or as "freaks" of nature. To him, on the contrary, the fact that they extended beyond the probability factor indicated that some *causal* principle must be at work.

In Jung's view the results of Rhine's experiments do not indicate the need for an explanatory principle within the limits of causality, but rather underscore the fact that cause-and-effect categories cannot adequately comprehend the phenomena of the psyche. The aspect of the experiments that is of the greatest importance to Rhine himself is the statistical verification indicating that parapsychic effects are beyond the element of chance. This turns out to be of considerable, albeit indirect, value to Jung. Jung had not felt the need to prove statistically the existence of a class of phenomena that he had observed time and again in the course of his work with the unconscious. Nevertheless, the fact that Rhine made his demonstration with the use of modern laboratory methods and with "scientific safeguards" that have been adequate to withstand attack on statistical grounds, is of course important in validating the appearance of the phenomena within an academic context.

At this point Jung made the general observation that a main aspect of the principle of causality as it has come to be used in modern science is that its laws are *statistical* laws. The implication of this is that they are valid only as long as they remain within a given range of probability. Statistical laws are not true absolutely, but only *essentially* or *mostly* true. That part of the phenomena that does not fit within the absolute statement of the law—in other words, those events that constitute the statistical variables—do not indicate that the causal principle is not valid in itself, but rather that *another principle of interpretation* may be necessary *as well.* In offering Synchronicity as a principle of interpretation, Jung does not intend it as a substitute for causality, but only as an additional and complementary principle. He is seeking to fill in the open spaces left by statistical laws.

The fact that Rhine's experiments with parapsychic events actually went beyond the probability factor is taken by Jung as evidence of the need for a synchronistic principle of interpretation to balance causality. He expressed this thought very clearly in his introduction to the English edition of the *I Ching*, in the passage to which we referred earlier. "Since the latter (Causality) is a merely statistical truth and not absolute, it is a sort of working hypothesis of how events evolve one out of another, whereas synchronicity takes the coincidence of events in space and time as meaning something more than mere chance; namely, a peculiar interdependence of objective events among themselves as well as with the subjective (psychic) states of the observer or observers."[1] This is the meaning of Jung's statement that Rhine's work has furnished "decisive evidence for the existence of acausal combinations of events."[2]

The criterion for comparing the two evaluations of Rhine's experiments—Rhine's causative and Jung's synchronistic—is that when we adopt Jung's point of view we are in a better position to frame hypotheses

[1] *I Ching, Op Cit.,* p. XXIV.
[2] C. G. Jung, *Synchronicity.* Op. cit., p. 431, 432.

regarding the phenomena and to participate more deeply in the underlying spirit of parapsychic events. We can see this more specifically now when we turn to examine the way Jung applies his conception of Synchronicity, utilizing the perspective of the Self and the archetypes to provide a context for understanding those psychic events that go beyond our present causalistic principles.

In approaching this subject, Jung first examined the basis for the affirmative results that Rhine obtained in his experiments. Some characteristics of the experiments emerge quite clearly. A first and very significant point is that the results of the tests on individuals were uneven. Some were negative insofar as the number of correct "guesses" was below probability. On the other hand, other tests went far beyond the probability figure. In this regard, the conclusion seems to suggest itself that certain individuals—perhaps certain "types" of individuals—are better able to function in the parapsychic situation. There is a strong indication that temperamental endowment or other such individual factors—perhaps they may best be summed up as the quality of sensitivity to the unconscious—play an important role in parapsychic perception.

There seems, however, in addition to this to have been a subjective factor of another kind at work in Rhine's experiments. This factor is of great importance and involves the *interest* that the person took in the test. A great deal depended on the sense of relationship that the person felt toward the experiments as a whole. The medium Eileen Garrett, for example, had obtained significantly affirmative results on other occasions; but she was not able to establish a sense of rapport because of the impersonality of the laboratory conditions, and so her results were negative. On the whole, those persons who entered into the experiments with a belief in the value of the work and especially with a hopeful attitude for the success of the tests, tended to have better scores. They apparently contributed something of their own psychic selves to the work.

It was found also that as the tests proceeded and as the novelty of the experiments settled down into routine, the initial enthusiasm began to wane. At that point the percentage of correct guesses grew smaller and smaller. This was true even of those individuals who remained sanguine about the evperiments and retained a strong desire to see them succeed. The factor of interest, while involving the subjective point of view of the person, apparently operated according to a definite pattern.

Jung's judgment on this basis is that if Rhine had not used a great variety of individuals in his tests, his results would have been significantly less affirmative. The greater the number of individuals taking part in the test, the more the composite score would be increased by the *new interest* generated by the novelty of enterprise in each new participant. Had a small number of individuals carried through the same total number of tries, Jung feels that the results would have been significantly different. Nonetheless, this would not have weakened the basic validity of Rhine's experiments. It would rather have underscored the importance of the "interest" factor, which, indirectly, gives a main clue to the principles underlying parapsychic phenomena.[1]

Before following up the importance of the interest factor and its significance in a depth psychological perspective, we should note that physical energy seems not to be a crucial factor in producing parapsychological effects. At first sight, it would seem that the importance of the individual's interest in the experiments would indicate an intensification in the psychic energy available for the work. It may be thought that this energy somehow affects the accuracy of the guesses, although it is not easy to conceive how this can be so. One set of Rhine's experiments, however, clearly eliminates an energy hypothesis. These were the experiments conducted at great distances, the participants being in one case 960 miles and in another case 4,000 miles apart at the time of the experiment. The results in both cases were significantly affirmative so that Rhine states that "A review of the thousands of cases in the Duke collection shows *no relationship* at all between distance and the number or type of psychic experiences."[2]

Jung's comment on these results is that "The fact that distance has no effect in principle shows that the thing in question cannot be a phenomenon of force

[1] Ibid., p. 434, 435.
[2] J. B. Rhine, *New World of the Mind*. New York: William Sloane Associates, p. 16.

or energy. . . . We have no alternative but to assume that distance is psychically variable, and may in certain circumstances be reduced to vanishing point by a psychic condition."[1] In other words, the primary factor is not the sum of energy psychologically generated, but rather the general condition established in the psyche as a whole. If energy could be shown to have a bearing on parapsychic events, then to that extent the principles of cause and effect would have to be applied. Since this is apparently not so, however, "it seems more likely," as Jung says, "that scientific explanation will have to begin with a criticism of our concepts of space and time on the one hand, and with the unconscious on the other."[2]

The classic, affirmative results that Rhine obtained must be classified as a kind of perception. It is clear, nevertheless, that they are not based on observation in our usual sense of the term, for they do not involve actual visual contact. It is a perception, rather, that proceeds directly from the unconscious with no conscious mediation, not even with any overt contact with the object. The act of naming the card, in Jung's words, "is not the result of his observing the physical cards, it is a product of pure imagination, of 'chance' ideas which reveal the structure of that which produces them, namely the unconscious."[3]

The phrase "pure imagination" as Jung uses it here is rather misleading. Jung does not mean that the

---

[1] C. G. Jung. *Synchronicity*. Op. cit., p. 433.
[2] Ibid., p. 435.
[3] Ibid., p. 436.

process of "reading" the symbols on the cards is a matter of fancy. He means rather that since there is no mediation of sensory perception or of conscious thoughts, the entire process takes place within the realm of the unconscious. The question that is crucial, then, is to determine what actually occurs in the unconscious on such occasions. It appears from the wide variations in Rhine's results that what takes place in the unconscious is not always the same. The cases recording the highest percentage of correct answers were those in which there was a great intensity of interest, with the added fact that the best results came at the beginning of the tests when the subject's interest was still at its highest. The primary characteristic of the successful results, then, was that they coincided with an exceedingly affirmative condition of the psyche, a condition in which the psyche was pervaded by an attitude of hopeful expectancy.

Jung has referred to the parapsychic phenomena of the Rhine laboratories as being based on the archetypal quality of hope. This is one of the points upon which Jung elaborated by writing a paragraph of explanation on the back of a page of the original manuscript. He referred me to page 26 of the German edition of his book on Synchronicity and then expanded his point about the relation of hope to the archetypal processes that are the vehicles through which the Synchronicity principle is manifested. "The test person," he wrote, "either *doubts* the possibility of knowing something one cannot know, or *hopes* that it will be possible and that the miracle will happen. At all events the test person being confronted with a seemingly impossible task finds himself in the archetypal situation, which so often occurs in myths and fairy tales, where a divine intervention, i.e., a miracle, offers the only solution."[1]

At another place in my manuscript, writing in the margin of a page and inserting his words between the lines of the text, Jung carried this comment further and made it more explicit. He said that, rather than speak of an archetype of hope, he would prefer to speak of the "archetype of the miracle," or the archetype of "magic effect." To understand what Jung has in mind when he uses such a phrase, we must bear in mind the active quality that he finds in the archetypal level of experience. Archetypes are not abstract universal images. They are effective factors that bring about processes of change at profound levels of the human psyche.

When Jung refers to "the archetype of the miracle" or of "magic effect," he is giving a name to the particular quality of expectation that human beings intuitively feel with respect to the capacity that the life process possesses to bring about changes in its own functioning. Mankind has always sensed that experiences taking place on the archetypal level have the power to change things. They have called such change by various names, from the divine to the demonic. But primary has been the quality of expectation that is associated with such power. It is uncanny, and

[1] For a reproduction of this comment as Jung wrote it, see page 107.

magical, and it becomes a source of strong belief because it fascinates man in the sense that it transfixes his consciousness. Thus it has an hypnoidal effect, and leads to faiths of great psychic intensity, which are then clothed in the various cultural symbolisms of religion and mythology. These faiths are based on, and operate in terms of, man's intuitive belief in the power of the archetypal force to affect life in mysterious ways. The particular patterns of such beliefs Jung calls *the archetype of magical effect.*

When we think back to the fundamental division in Jung's schematization of the psyche—the division between the Personal Unconscious and the Collective, or Transpersonal, Unconscious—we realize that the experiences of the archetype of the miracle, or of magical effect, take place at the most fundamental level of the psyche. Much deeper than the personal, it has its effect at the *transpersonal* level. This is the operational significance of Jung's using the phrase, "pure imagination." He wished to emphasize the fact that personal factors are not significantly involved in the objectivity of the laboratory situation. The success of parapsychological experiments like those that Rhine conducted, therefore, depend on the attitude of intense hopefulness and anticipation generated by the archetype of magical effect in modern and primitive man alike.

Jung's point is that, while the mere fact of guessing the symbols on cards is a simple and rather objective human act, the process itself activates something at the archetypal level of the psyche when the individ-

cp. Synchronicidet p. 26.

The test person either doubts the possibility
of knowing something, one cannot know, or
hopes, that it will be possible, and that the
miracle will happen. At all events the test-
person being confronted with a seemingly impossible task so finds himself in the arch-
typal situation, which so often occurs in Myth
and Fairy Tale, where a divine intervention, i.e,
a miracle offers the only solution.

PLATE 1   On Hope and Parapsychology

107

ual approaches it and experiences it with intensity.
Further, while the process of impersonal expectation
of the miracle is archetypal, it contains a root of in-
stinctuality. This leads back even beyond the archetype to the primal points at which instinct and archetype are united as opposites in the primary patterns
of human behavior. It leads back to what Jung describes as the *psychoid* factor. What is involved in
the archetype of magic effect is thus a *psychoid* process, primitive in its simplicity and touching the deepest, most fundamental aspects of the psyche.[1]

The question arises, then, of how the involvement
of a psychoid process brings parapsychic events to
pass. In treating this subject, Jung makes use of a
deceptively simple psychological conception that he
derives from Pierre Janet and refers to as the partial
abaissement du niveau mental, a partial "lowering of
the mental level." The word "partial" is important
for understanding the process because the "lowering"
that takes place on one side of the psyche is preceded
by a "heightening" on the other side.

The process involved here is related to Jung's conception of "numinosity," which he uses to describe
the aura of great light and also of great warmth that
is attached to the archetypes when they become directly manifest in a strong human experience. Numinosity is an expression of great psychic intensity.

---

[1] The interpretation that I am presenting here is based on several
detailed conversations with Professor Jung, centering on this point
and reflecting his view that his original statement is too open to
misinterpretation.

When a numinous event occurs, therefore, it draws a large concentration of psychic energy around it. This energy constellates around the archetypal symbol that is active as the effective center of the experience. A *complex*, or *cluster*, of psychic contents is thus formed at this point. As the energies available to the psyche are drawn together in one part of the psyche, the other areas are left more or less depleted.

There follows a lowering of the mental level on that side of the psyche from which energy has been withdrawn. The contents of this side sink downward into the lower levels of the unconscious. While the level of conscious activity is heightened and intensified on one side of the psyche, the conscious controls are altogether loosened on the other side so that the psyche is open to the full impact of archetypal factors at the deepest level, especially the psychoid level, of the unconscious. As Jung puts it, "Owing to the restriction of consciousness produced by the affect so long as it lasts, there is a corresponding lowering of orientation which in its turn gives the unconscious a favorable opportunity to slip into the space vacated. Thus we regularly find that unexpected or otherwise inhibited unconscious contents break through and find expression in the affect."[1]

To understand what happens when parapsychic events occur, we have to hold in our minds a conception of the *dynamic balancing process* by which the psyche functions. When consciousness is intensified

[1] Ibid., p. 436, 437.

on one side of the psyche, it is lowered on the other side, and the two events take place at the same time as part of a single process. Significantly, it is the heightening of consciousness that leads to a corresponding lowering, and through this lowering the capacities of awareness are expanded. This awareness is expressed directly via the unconscious, since it does not follow the processes by which knowledge customarily enters consciousness. It presents itself as knowledge that comes *without* the medium of consciousness. This is what gives it its parapsychic aspect, and it is this that makes extrasensory perception so significant a phenomenon. It indicates the presence of a capacity for knowledge that is latent in the unconscious, and that can operate without intermediaries. It indicates an ability in man that has been developed only to a small degree but that involves the capacity of making specific kinds of cognition *directly accessible* to the psyche. The specific means by which such direct cognition without the intervention of consciousness takes place is difficult to delineate in detail because its forms are so variable and unpredictable. It becomes present in different ways at different times, since it involves as great a diversity as the means by which knowledge comes through consciousness in its ordinary forms.

On the basis of the concepts that have been described, we can now present at least the general format of an interpretation of unconscious cognition. The intensification of an archetypal content in consciousness brings about a "lowering of the mental level" on the other side of the psyche. Through this, the unconscious is made more easily susceptible to outside influences. It becomes as if more sensitive.

(Note: In my original manuscript, this last sentence read simply, "It becomes more sensitive." When he read it in 1954, Jung crossed that out and rewrote it in pencil as, "It becomes as if more sensitive." I have let the change stand, recognizing the reasons for which he made it. The modification that he inserted has a significance that is well worth noting.)

As the factors inhibiting the perceptive power of the unconscious are diminished, whatever capacities of cognition are resting latent in the unconscious tend to be expressed on the surface of the psyche. The lowering of the mental level draws the functioning of that side of the psyche down to the deeper level of the unconscious. This is the level that Jung calls *psychoid*, meaning that it is only psychelike, not yet psyche. It is at so primal a level that the process of differentiation into the opposites of life has not yet been carried through. Thus, in its psychoid form, the distinct aspects of the psyche have not yet been separated from one another, as archetype and instinct, body and mind.

In Jung's scheme of thought, the *psychoid* level of the unconscious represents the point at which the psyche is so close to the animal world as not yet to be differentiated from it. It still is directly connected to the realm of nature in its mode of functioning, and it is thus the aspect of the human organism that can be most directly experienced as a part of nature. On the one hand we are able to deal with the specific aspects of this in empirical terms by means of the concepts of biology and psychology. On the other hand, and much more fundamentally, our individual contact with the psychoid level of our human nature involves an inner experience of the deep ground of the Self experienced subjectively within ourselves and also objectively as part of the whole realm of nature.

We see in this the twofold conception of the Self that is basic in the structure of Jung's thinking. On one level, the Self is an evolutionary concept, emerging from nature and providing the ground of reality that underlies the development of the human individual as a member of the species. As such, the Self is empirical, insofar as it comprises the base for all the phenomena that the sciences of man undertake to study. In this sense, the reality of the Self is reality with a small r.

The second level of Jung's conception of the Self, however, is more ontological than empirical. The nature of its reality here must be spelled with a capital R, just as the Self itself must be spelled with a capital S. It is here the ultimate reality of being. The Self conceived in this larger sense is the equivalent of Leibniz's "pre-established harmony" or of the Tao. It is the encompassing unity *in* which and *by means of* which the macrocosm and the microcosm participate in each other, and specifically by which the ultimate realities of the universe are expressed and reflected in the life of the human individual.[1]

We can restate the formulation that Jung reached in his later years with respect to the strata of the psyche. He separated it finally into four levels that enabled him to describe operationally the various types of human cognition. At the surface is *Ego Consciousness*. The *Personal Unconscious* is just below it. Beneath that, extending for a considerable depth, is the transpersonal level of the *Collective Unconscious*. And at the base is the *Psychoid* level, reaching into the realm of nature itself.

The process of which we have spoken as the "lowering" of the mental level takes place through the intensification of the archetypal contents and the consequent drawing of large sums of psychic energy into consciousness. Its primary effect is that it opens the very deep stratum of the Self, the Psychoid, to whatever factors are present in the continuum of the Self. In this condition the Psychoid level of the psyche is open to influences of every possible kind. It is accessible to whatever forces and factors happen to be present at a given moment in the continuum of the Self, whether these are factors operating within one's own psyche, within the psyche of others, or whether they are forces of any other kind active in the universe.

Considering this, we recognize that in opening the individual at the psychoid level, the process of mental

[1] For a fuller discussion of this aspect of Jung's thinking see Progoff, *The Death and Rebirth of Psychology*, Ch. VI, especially Part 2, "The Self as Symbol and Reality," p. 177.

abaissement makes a person psychically vulnerable at the same time that it greatly enlarges the range of his psychic possibilities. The specific effect upon him depends on the nature of the other factors and influences that are present in the continuum of the Self within the range of his personal atmosphere. They may be affirmative or negative, beneficial or destructive; they may assist the life of a person, or they may distract from it by giving false leadings and confusions.

Each experience has to be appraised on its own merits, especially since its effect upon an individual depends a great deal upon the state of inner development within that person. In principle, the factors that exert influence during the condition of *abaissement* are of the greatest diversity. They may range from petty subjective anxieties to large visionary awarenesses of prophetic scope. They may reflect some small cranny of an individual microcosm, or they may reflect the large wisdom of the macrocosm. Any of them may be reflected at the psychoid level when *abaissement* takes place.

In this respect, Leibniz's perspective is especially relevant and his description of what takes place is most expressive. In his words, the human being as a "monad" is a "perpetual living mirror of the universe." Within this framework, it seems clear that Jung's analysis is spelling out the psychological phenomonology by which this process of "mirroring" takes place. With the conception of Synchronicity and its psychological foundation in the Self, we begin to have a basis on which to proceed, and a framework in which to formulate descriptive concepts. Once the functioning of a significant part of the psyche has dropped to the psychoid depth, the individual, as microcosm, is in a condition at which a part of his psyche is able to "catch" the "reflections" of the surrounding macrocosm to describe them and make them articulate.

To speak of this *direct presentation* of the surrounding world in terms of macrocosm and microcosm is to set it in its most general and abstract context. As it is experienced by individuals in the actuality of their lives, it always involves the specific circumstances of a given moment of time. At each moment throughout the universe, a *pattern of being* prevails in which all the monads, or individual beings, are interlocked with each other, each reflecting unconsciously in themselves (latently and very seldom articulately) the entirety of the pattern that contains them. Each of these patterns represents the condition of "harmony" or "Tao" as constellated throughout the universe at a given moment. When the "lowering of the mental level" increases the sensitivity of the psyche to the reflections of the pattern, the individual becomes capable of perception or cognition that goes beyond space and time in our usual causalistic sense.

One significant group of the phenomena that are classified as "parapsychic" consists apparently of those psychoid experiences in which various aspects of the pattern of a moment of time are reflected to an individual by means of subliminal perceptions of which he himself may not be aware. These "reflections" take place in unconscious forms, as is inherent in the fact that they are occurring at the psychoid level. They may appear in hypnosis, in dreams, in trance, or in other variations of the mediumistic state. All of them depend upon the condition of *abaissement* and the depth to which it has been established.

Abaissement may be brought about deliberately by specific disciplines and techniques, or it may happen spontaneously and involuntarily without an individual's realizing what is taking place. Especially in the latter cases, where the occurrence of synchronistic events is reflected in an individual's psyche and is experienced by him as a parapsychic phenomenon, the unconsciousness of the experience may have a very confusing effect. This is one reason, I believe, in addition to the generally unsettling effects of *abaissement*, why many of the people who are classed in the category of psychics tend to be subject to periods of instability and mental confusion. They experience great difficulty in understanding the nature of the synchronistic phenomena that are being perceived. It is difficult for them to distinguish which are to be assimilated into their lives and which are not relevant for them.

This is a further reason why it is important for us to enlarge our understanding of what synchronistic phenomena involve. Not recognizing the nature of the synchronistic principle that is working in them, people very easily project their favorite symbol or doctrine into the experiences of this kind that come to them. Thus they add to the infinity of occult dogmas and further confuse their personal experience. The Synchronicity hypothesis, however, can enable a person to clarify what is taking place in many of his parapsychic perceptions. Thus it can enable psychically sensitive persons to find their bearings in their lives, especially when it is used in the context of a full life-development program.

While the Synchronicity principle deals with the patterning of experience across a moment of time, there seems to be a variability in the units of time that are involved. There is some indication that the parapsychic perception of synchronistic events does not always reflect the pattern of the then existing moment of time. Various researches, those of Dunne and Soal among others, have suggested the possibility that in the mirroring of patterns that takes place, what is reflected may refer either to the past or to the future. Should this be so, it would not alter but rather expand the basic conception that parapsychic events involve the mirroring via the deeper levels of the psyche of other, separate, and causally unrelated events, which nevertheless belong to the same patterning of time.

In those cases where Rhine's experiments obtained results beyond the factor of probability, the effective principle was that an archetypal psychic process involving hopeful expectancy was made intensely active by the early interest felt by those participants in the tests. This factor of hopefulness expressing the archetype of magical effect is often present in parapsychological experiments, probably because the persons who volunteer for them tend to be motivated by a strong desire to demonstrate to the scientific world the existence of an additional dimension of reality. The intensity brought about by this desire results in an *abaissement* on one side of the psyche and through this, mirrorings, or unconscious perceptions, reflecting *across* the pattern of the moment, occur. These come together into a meaningful conformity, a harmonious correspondence with the situation surrounding the archetype that had become active.

It seems fair to assume that in the continuity of the Rhine experiments or of other parapsychological experiments of that type, the total effect of the archetypal factors is at a minimum because of the cold atmosphere of objectivity deliberately maintained in the laboratory. Only the enthusiasm generated prior to entering the laboratory, the desire for the success of the experiment can be considered to be a factor stimulating enough to produce an *abaissement* in the psyche.

Outside of the laboratory, however, in the ordinary course of life in society, where the passions of belief have much freer reign, the area in which archetypal factors can be expressed is much greater. There is therefore every reason to believe that the incidence of parapsychic phenomena is of much greater scope outside laboratory conditions. This aspect of parapsychological research has been increasingly recognized in recent years, most notably in the emphasis placed by Gardner Murphy on the importance of "spontaneous experiences" in the study of parapsychological phenomena.

To speak of "spontaneous experiences" implies the recognition that parapsychic events take place primarily in the flux of our everyday lives. That is certainly the conclusion at which Jung arrived on the basis of his therapeutic work as a depth psychologist. His studies also of many religions impressed him with the relationship between the symbols at the archetypal level of the psyche and the various experiences of the miraculous that have occurred throughout religious history. There is considerable reason to think that the phenomena of *abaissement* occur much more readily in social situations where the emotionality of crowds and traditions and faiths are at work, than it does in individuals alone. In a minor form, the testing environment of the parapsychology laboratory provides such a social situation, as also the expectation of their "clients" draws forth "spiritual" results from clairvoyants and mediums.

The social effect of activating the archetypes and bringing about *abaissement* is clearly indicated by the fact that there are significantly more parapsychic phenomena taking place and being reported now in 1973 than in 1954 when this paper was originally written. The change in social atmosphere is the primary reason for this. It activates the psychoid level with beliefs and expectations and provides a permissive atmosphere in which increasingly it has become socially acceptable for individuals to report their parapsychic experiences.

In previous decades, not only the reports but the experiences themselves were repressed. Now the social atmosphere draws forth these experiences and is creating a cultural openness in which specifically parapsychic phenomena as well as the larger realm of synchronistic events as a whole can more freely be experienced, observed, and reported. In this atmosphere also the capacity for this larger range of experience can be cultivated by specific techniques of training, as well as by an affirmative orientation to the experiences themselves. By means of this, the quality of awareness in our culture as a whole will steadily be enlarged.

In a social climate that is conducive to those experiences that involve a contact with the deep levels of the Self, it becomes possible to do the experimentation that is necessary in order to improve the techniques by which *abaissement* can be brought about. In this work, two factors are of primary consideration. One is the importance of spontaneity; the other is the social circumstances in which parapsychic events take place.

Spontaneity, even to the degree of absolute surprise, is an element that is inherent in authentic synchronistic events. Because the unpremeditatedness of spontaneity is one of the distinguishing characteristics of synchronistic events, parapsychic research must find means of studying the phenomena that take place in the midst of unplanned life experience. This implies the necessity of studying the varieties of synchronistic events as they are brought about under the impact of social life. Studies of this kind will lead to an understanding of parapsychic and synchronistic phenomena and thus will yield a fuller insight into the way that cultural change is brought about.

Synchronistic events in particular hold an important clue to those "miraculous" occurrences that become the basis for religious traditions and mythologies. Even the events of political history, we may find, depend a great deal on parapsychic sensitivity as well as on the capacity of charismatic persons to generate the atmosphere in which synchronistic events, ranging from faith healing to perfect political timing, can come to pass. All of these depend upon the role of the archetypal factors, the *abaissement* of the mental level, and the activation of the psychoid depths of the Self so that the mirroring of parapsychic and synchronistic phenomena can take place.

IX The Operation of Synchronicity

In order to provide a context wide enough to comprehend the synchronistic foundations of parapsychic phenomena—synchronistic events being the more inclusive category—it has been necessary to keep our discussion up to this point on a generally abstract level. Now, however, we can approach the phenomena more directly as they are experienced, to see how the psyche and its archetypes are involved.

We find the synchronistic principle expressed in a very wide variety of events. A person, for example, has a dream or a series of dreams, and these turn out to coincide with an outer event. An individual prays for some special favor, or wishes, or hopes for it strongly, and in some inexplicable way it comes to pass. One person believes in another person, or in some special symbol, and while he is praying or meditating by the light of that faith, a physical healing or some other "miracle" comes to pass. Wherever there are human beings, synchronistic events occur, and it is indeed very likely that once we know what to look for, we shall find that their number is much greater than we had supposed.

In all such events a strong archetypal factor is at work in a numinous way. Dreams that give a knowledge beyond what is available to consciousness necessarily involve images that lie deep in the psyche. The belief in the power of the wish reaches far into the primitive mind of man. It is the key to the effectiveness of the primordial image of the magician. The fundamental experience of faith, whatever the form or object, always touches the profoundest levels of the unconscious. Because this is so, an emotional intensity is generated around the numinous, archetypal factor and results in a corresponding withdrawal of energy, a lowering of the mental level on the other side of the psyche. Here we have the psychological mechanism of *abaissement* by which the psyche is brought to reflect the patterns of time. By recognizing this, the individual is able to bring himself into relation with the Synchronicity of events.

Now, however, an interesting question arises. In this analysis of what takes place in the psyche of a person who is participating in a parapsychic or other synchronistic situation, the importance ascribed to the archetypal factor has centered on the role of the archetype in bringing about a partial lowering of the mental level. We notice also that synchronistic events tend to reflect the characteristics of the operative archetype. It seems very much as if the archetype plays an important role in constellating the pattern, so that the pattern that forms is somehow in the image of the archetype.

Jung states it as his experience that parapsychic events "nearly always occur in the region of archetypal constellations, that is, in situations which have either activated an archetype or were called up by the autonomous action of an archetype."[1] The intensity of the archetype apparently sets up a situation that has its own requirements and characteristics, and these characteristics are expressed in the pattern that forms at a moment of time when the archetype becomes effective. The psychic reflections in the Self that come about through the "lowering of the mental level" shape themselves into a form that corresponds to the archetype.

The implication thus arises, at least on first consideration, that if the influence of the archetype determines the pattern of the events that follow upon its being activated in a numinous way, we must really speak of it in terms of causality. The problem is indeed significant because, even if we say that the numinosity of the archetype involves an intangible "magical power," we are still imputing causality to the events. Jung quite aptly uses the phrase "magic causality" to describe this point of view. There is no question but that certain elements of it are found in the Synchronicity principle, or at least in the think-

[1] See his discussion of the "Astrological Experiment." Ibid., pp. 480–483.

ing that leads to Synchronicity. This is in fact shown concretely when Jung refers to some writings of Albertus Magnus in which the factor of emotionality is referred to as creating an intense one-sidedness in the psyche; and this is then considered to be the basic prerequisite for a magical effect.

Jung quotes Albertus Magnus as saying that everyone can influence everything magically if he "falls into a great excess."[1] Essentially, this expresses the same idea that Jung developed on the basis of Pierre Janet, the *abaissement* of the mental level. The "excess" of which Albertus Magnus speaks is the intensity of feeling, the passion of faith or of desire that overtakes a person, and thereby "tips" the balance in his psyche. There is, however, an important difference.

Jung's analysis of *abaissement* is intended primarily to describe the process by which the transition takes place from one pattern across time to another, and especially by which the second pattern is experienced and perceived. In the case of "magic causality" the factor of emotionality does not remain objective. Even though the entire process takes place deep in the unconscious, an egoistic factor is involved and the "will" attached to the emotional affect is thought to be purposive and causative in nature.

In the case of the practicing magician, of whom Albertus Magnus was speaking, the will belongs to the individual who deliberately falls into "the state of excess" through which his emotionality can alter

[1] Ibid., p. 448.

events. In the case of the primitives, the "will" may belong to any object as an aspect of its special spiritual potency, the divine or magic power that may be ascribed to it. When the primitive believes that the presence of a certain animal, for example, will have an effect on the affairs of the tribe, it is not merely a matter of imputation, nor altogether of suggestion. The belief in the magical potency of the animal is derived from a larger symbol drawn from the myths of the culture, a symbol of an historical and archetypal nature that is projected upon the animal.

The animal, or other object or person, thus unwittingly participates in a large scheme of meaning whose basis lies in the unconscious of the primitive. The act of seeing the individual animal constellates the entire archetype and results in changes in the emotional intensity and psychic equilibrium; and this, in turn, both reflects and is reflected in a new pattern or orderedness of the events across time.[1]

In the ancient Teutonic mythology, the belief in the capacity of a wishing rod or other wishing objects to make wishes come true rests upon a similar foundation.[2] Wishing involves an intensification of emotion, and the force of this energy brings about a new patterning in the situation *across* time.

We must note also that the fact of this intense wishing is in itself part of a new patterning of time. The effectiveness of the emotionality of wishing caused it

[1] Ibid., p. 482, 483.
[2] Ibid., p. 517.

to be classified as a "divine power" by the Teutons, as it is also considered to be by other peoples. We must also point out, however, that wishing is never believed to be effective when it is done haphazardly. It must be done according to some historically prescribed ritual or within some fundamental symbol, for only then can an archetype be activated. The presence of an archetype as an effective factor is crucial for the entire process, for it is only by means of an archetype that the principle of the acausal patterning of events can begin to apply.

In all such situations, whether we think of them in terms of magic causality or of Synchronicity, there are two elements that need to be related. One is the series of events taking place within the human psyche. These proceed in a chain of interior causation including the activation of the archetype, the intensification of emotion, and the consequent lowering of the mental level. The other element is the "arrangement of an external and independent event" taking place outside the psyche.[1] The question is whether we can find any direct link between the two to show that one, particularly the psychic, brings the other, the outer condition, into being.

Those points of view that accept magic causality have no difficulty in placing such a construction on events because they postulate a divine or demonic power in order to explain the changes that take place across the patterns of time. The psyche is then treated

[1] Ibid., p. 482.

as though it has acted as an effective causative agent, whether it has done so emotionally through the unconscious or through the conscious ego by means of "will power."

Jung's thinking on this point is subtle and very elusive. The significance of his formulation can very easily be missed. On the one hand, his constant emphasis in describing the archetypes is that they have the power to do things, that they are numinous, and have a *wirkend* ("vital" or "efficient") power that brings things to pass. On the other hand, the essence of his larger conception is that the archetypes do not function in terms of cause and effect. As a matter of fact, it was precisely when he realized that the archetypes obey something other than causality that he felt the need to study the possibility of an alternate principle. Thus he was led to formulate the hypothesis of Synchronicity.

In order to understand the principle behind this apparent contradiction, we must bear in mind the larger perspective in which Synchronicity is conceived as a principle functioning in the macrocosm as a whole. The patterns that are formed synchronistically across a moment of time encompass the entire universe. This is true as a general principle, and from the philosophic side it refers back to Leibniz. Within this general context, however, we have the individual beings who participate in the pattern, whose lives and actions express it.

The individual microcosmic life is an aspect of the larger general pattern of the macrocosm. Nonetheless, the individual who is engaged in expressing the macrocosmic pattern that encompasses him is doing so by actions in his life that are apparently decided rationally. He moves toward consciously determined goals, and proceeds toward his goals on the basis of cause-and-effect thinking.

The unfoldment of a human life is thus taking place on two distinct planes, simultaneously on two separate dimensions of reality. The one is the individual's perceptions of his life, his motivations, and his actions. It takes place by means of thought and emotion, and it moves toward perceivable goals on the assumption of cause and effect, whether it conceives cause and effect in modern rationalistic terms or in the animistic terms of primitive magic.

The second dimension, on the other hand, is more than individual. It is the transpersonal macrocosmic field in which Synchronicity operates. Within this field, which encompasses the patterning of the universe across time at each specific moment of time, there are, as Jung says, "certain regularities and therefore constant factors."[1] It is these regularities that Jung is seeking to clarify when he analyzes the various characteristics of the archetypes, their numinosity, the ways in which they are activated, their effect in upsetting the equilibrium of the psyche, and their constellative quality in drawing other psychic contents into complexes around them.

All these factors proceed in a regular and describ-

[1] Ibid., p. 516.

able, in principle predictable, manner. Each of them has a specific chain of causality, and to that degree, its past can be understood in causal terms. So also can its future be understood; but this is only within the context of each specific line of causality that is moving in the continuity of its life. As soon as we have more than one line of causality coming together with another, something more than causality is called into play. The direct effects of the interaction of one upon the other can certainly be understood in terms of causality. When many lines of causal history come together at a given moment, however, a pattern of multiples is formed. These may interact upon one another, and to the degree that they do so, what may be called a cross-causality of interaction takes place. In the largest percentage of cases, however, there is no cross-causality because there is no interaction.

There is also, in the vast majority of cases, no direct relationship between the various individual conditions that are established at a given moment of time. Each is there in that particular form at that particular moment because of its own causal reasons. The unique history of each has brought it there, and the fact that any two are there together at that particular moment is a matter of coincidence from the causal point of view. There are occasions, however, when events that are not causally related to one another take place at the same time in a way that is so filled with meaning that it seems to hold more than coincidence. In a word, it seems to be *meaningful.*

It is these events of *meaningful coincidence* that

Jung sees as the essence of Synchronicity. Significantly, when Jung was reading the above paragraph in my original manuscript, he felt the need to elaborate my statement by adding examples and writing in his penciled longhand on the back of the preceding page a substantial explanatory comment. That comment is valuable as an addition and clarification of Jung's thinking on Synchronicity, and it is also indicative of the intense personal involvement that Jung brought to this subject. I quote it as he wrote it, and it is reproduced on p. 133.

Jung wrote: "All these regular processes are *causal*, therefore relatively or in principle predictable. Synchronicity comes into consideration only in the case of two or more causal chains running parallel to each other and representing the same meaning; for example, I am thinking, how the chthonic spirit (Serpens Mercurii) overcomes and integrates the Christian symbol (fish) and I see a real snake catching and swallowing a fish. *There is no causal connection*, or little as in precognition, where I foresee something, which is going to happen several months later. One cannot assume that a future event can have a causal effect in the present."

When two or more events take place at a given moment of time without either one having caused the other but with a distinctly meaningful relationship existing between them beyond the possibilities of coincidence, that situation has the basic elements of Synchronicity. Events of this type usually involve different individuals or groups. We find this to be the case in the synchronistic occurrences that take place in interpersonal relationships; and it is even more markedly so in the events of history. Sometimes, in addition, two distinct noncausally connected sequences of events come together within a single individual and meet in his life in a way that is meaningful beyond coincidence. Conditions in the mind or body may be examples of this, as we see in the fact that both illness and "spontaneous" healings may be understood as examples of Synchronicity in certain instances. The same is true of several classifications of events that are now being studied in the field of parapsychology.

From an analytic and interpretive point of view, the situation that is set up by his hypothesis of the Synchronicity principle is very frustrating to Jung. Since it includes no fixed causal connections, it has no room for prediction in the ordinary sense. One cannot do anything about it, neither to cause more synchronistic events to happen, nor to avoid them. By definition one cannot *cause* synchronistic events, but on the basis of observations in this area over the past twenty years, it does seem to me to be possible to develop in a person an increased sensitivity to synchronistic events, and especially a capacity to harmonize one's life with such occurrences.

Jung gives some hints and leadings in this direction in the course of his general writings. A side effect of some of his psychological procedures is that they are conducive to strengthening the sensitivity to synchronistic situations. Jung's primary concern, however,

All these regular processes are causal, there=
fore relatively or in principal predictable. S (synchron.)
comes into consideration only in the case of 2 or more causal chains running parallel to each other and representing
the same meaning, f.i. I am thinking, how the chthonic
spirit (serpens Mercurii) overcomes and integrates the
christian symbol (fish) and I see a real snake
catching and swallowing a fish. There is no causal
connection, as little as in precognition, where
I foresee something, which is going to happen
several months later. One cannot assume that
a future event can have a causal effect in the
present.

PLATE 2   On Coincidence Beyond Causality

lay in the theoretical development of the Synchronicity principle. Since my original study of Synchronicity with Jung, a substantial part of my own applied
research in psychotherapy and the processes of spiritual growth has been directed toward the development of techniques for enlarging the relationship to
the synchronistic range of experience. I leave discussion of those techniques, however, for another time
and place.

Jung's focus of study lies in identifying the events
and the underlying forces that operate in situations
of Synchronicity. Since there is no possibility of making predictions on the basis of general laws where
Synchronicity is concerned, he limits himself to trac-
ing the inner movement of Synchronistic events. He
does this, well aware of the danger that, as people observe the activation of archetypal symbols in the presence of Synchronistic events, they will erroneously
assume that they are seeing causality at work. The
highly misleading inference of causality is bound to
arise, Jung says, as soon as the observer "perceives the
archetypal background." Then "he is tempted to trace
the mutual assimilation of independent psychic and
physical processes back to a causal effect of the archetype, and thus to overlook the fact that they are
merely contingent." But, Jung adds, "this danger is
avoided if one regards Synchronicity as a special instance of general acausal orderedness."[1]

The role of the archetypes is not as a causal factor

1 Ibid., p. 516.

operating external to the contents of the sychronistic event, but rather as a factor of inner cohesion and integration. While the pattern existing in the universe at any moment of time is so vast in its contents that it is diffuse, the archetypes are the factors within the psyche of man that draw the relevant contents together in terms of their meaningfulness to the human being. In the synchronistic view of the universe, the archetypes play a mediating role. It is *via the archetypes* that the encompassing pattern that traverses a moment of time is cohered and separated into minor patterns that relate to the life of the individual person.

Out of the fullness of the macrocosm, special and definite patterns are constellated around the archetypes. The archetypes do not *cause* this. The situations form around them, but are not caused by them. The specific role of the archetypes in synchronistic phenomena seems to be to serve as the constellating hub of a situation across time, and to be the factor of inner orderedness that gives the distinctive *set* to the situation. Thus, while each of the particular components within a situation has been brought to the present moment of time by its own chain of causality, the archetypes provide an additional factor that works *after* the causal effects have taken place. This is the inner orderedness of the situation that is established in synchronistic relationship to those archetypes that are active at a given moment in a person's life having been activated by *abaissement* on the psychoid level.

The constellative effect of the archetypes in addition to causality is what brings about "meaningful co-incidences" that are more meaningful than mere statistical probability would allow. It is interesting to note that when he was writing his basic statement of the Synchronicity principle, Jung became very much involved in demonstrating his point by means of statistical data, but that the statistical work led him into one difficulty after another.

One aspect of the problem derived from the nature of the statistical experiment that he set up. It dealt with the chance astrological pairing of sun and moon in married couples, and was itself open to considerable question. This so-called "astrological experiment" became a time-consuming detour that was not essential to the main conception of Synchronicity. As it happened, the statisticians and mathematicians to whom the English publisher gave the task of checking the validity of the data found that they had serious reservations about this use of statistics. One consequence was that the English publication of Jung's book on Synchronicity was substantially delayed before an area of agreement among the mathematical professionals could be reached.

Jung was very annoyed by the delays, and especially by the nature of the queries and criticisms that were made of him. He felt that those critiques of his statistical work were made without an understanding of the inner meaning of the Synchronicity concept. Thus he wrote me in a letter dated January 7, 1955: "My essay on Synchronicity is not yet printed, as the expert for safe locks has not been able to open the barn door yet. I wonder why people so often labour under the impression that I could not possibly mean what I say."[1]

In another letter, dated September 11, 1954, and written to Dr. James Kirsch, Jung referred to this subject in a similar tone. He was commenting on how few people grasp the point of his Synchronicity thesis, adding the remark, "It is especially not understood what an excellent joke was made with the use of astrological statistics; people have even thought I wanted to prove something in favor of astrology; It is hardly worthwhile to deal with all this pack of nonsense."[2]

A curious factor of emotionality entered Jung's thinking where Synchronicity was concerned. When he was developing his other concepts, passions of various kinds also came into play, as is bound to be the case whenever a work of great originality is being created. The situation with Synchronicity, however, seems to have been qualitatively different from the time that he became seriously engaged in formulating the concept. So many frustrations entered the work that he began to feel that there was a "trickster" element at work in it. It seemed as though one of the playful gods who tease and play practical jokes on hu-

[1] The bottom part of that letter, which contains the material relevant to Synchronicity, is reproduced in Plate III, p. 138.

[2] James Kirsch. *Letters to a Friend*, This letter is reprinted in *Psychological Perspectives*, fall, 1972, Vol. 3, No. 2, p. 173. It was in this letter also that Jung recorded his first reading of the present manuscript, writing to Kirsch, "The other day I received a manuscript from Progoff, in which he discusses the question of Synchronicity very skillfully, especially under the aspect of archetypes."

As a matter of fact my books sell quite decently. That books like "Answer to Job" or "Synchronicity" should have a bad reception, is not astonishing, but my other books like Aion etc. are harmless enough. As scientific journals are occupied with their special interests, none cares for something, which is between the humanities and Natural science and between Medicine and Psychology. My essay on Synchronicity is not yet printed, as the expert for safe-locks has not been able to open the barn door yet. I wonder why people so often labour under the impression that I could not possibly mean what I say.

There is no point in wishing you a good trip across the ocean in our days, as it is now a mere hop, although an expensive one.

Yours cordially
C. G. Jung.

PLATE 3   On Statisticians and the Barn Door

138

man beings was tantalizing him.[1] At other times it seemed to him that Synchronicity had a spirit and a will of its own and that, in a demonic way, it created hurdles out of thin air in order to trip him. Reading his comment in his letter to Kirsch may, however, incline us to think that it was Jung himself who was playing the joke. He possessed an ample context in which to understand and absorb what was taking place; but it made him irritable nonetheless.

When his frustrations became particularly great, no matter how well he understood them, Jung was much like the rest of us in that he vented his vexations on those who were the bearers of his troubles. For a while, the statisticians played a scapegoat role in this way. In general, people who did not understand or appreciate the conception that he was trying to formulate and communicate at any given time caught the brunt of his impatience. Jung passed through periods like this in the course of developing his other concepts, but his intensity in the case of Synchronicity seems to have been the greatest.

One other book aroused a comparable amount of emotion in Jung, and that was his *Answer to Job*. It too was misunderstood and poorly accepted by the public at the time of its publication. Like his study of Synchronicity, it was a product of his later years and it culminated a major and very subtle line of his thought. Significantly, also, the theme of *Answer to Job* is a partial application of the Synchronicity prin-

[1] Paul Radin. *The Trickster,* with commentaries by Karl Kerenyi and C. G. Jung. New York: Philosophical Library, 1956.

ciple to theological issues, interpreting certain bibli-
cal events in a synchronistic context. In that book,
Jung was reaching out to lay claim to some of the vast
land that his vision of Synchronicity had enabled
him to see. Those first attempts were very difficult,
however.

The irritability in Jung where Synchronicity was
concerned can be understood and appreciated in
terms of the gap between the vastness of his vision
and the limits of what he could demonstrate and convey to the rationalistic minds of his generation. His
intuition enabled him to envision the principle of
Synchronicity as having applications throughout the
cosmos, and especially in all the areas where the
psyche of human beings is involved. But the range of
research and application this opened was so great,
while the task of formulating it and demonstrating it
was so difficult, that Jung felt himself to be caught
in the middle, surrounded by an unbridgeable gap
in communication.

Part of the difficulty and frustration that Jung experienced seems to have been related, however, to a
more basic question of content. It involved the question of the context in which Synchronicity can best be
understood. Is Synchronicity a principle of interpretation that is specifically related to the experience of
human beings? If so, it is a field of relevance that has
an enormous scope and application; but in that case,
it is a field that is definite and is limited to the presence of human life. The other possibility is that Synchronicity is a general principle of understanding

that is applicable to all the phenomena of nature. In that case, its relevance is for all the sciences as a whole, and not merely for those human sciences that deal with the phenomena and destiny of man's life.

At numerous points in Jung's writings and commentaries on Synchronicity, we find an ambiguity and unclearness where these possibilities are concerned. On the one hand, Jung's experience was primarily as a psychotherapist dealing exclusively with the lives of human beings. The data to which he had access was drawn from the varieties of human existence. In addition, the conceptions that he had developed and in which he had a special expertise, dealt with the deep and hidden processes of human development. His understanding of these provided the basis for his conception of Synchronicity, and we might therefore expect that the emphasis that Jung would choose for Synchronicity would be to place it primarily in the realm of human experience. The opposite was the case, however. Jung spent his greatest personal efforts in attempting to persuade not the psychologists but the physicists. His main dialogue in his last years regarding Synchronicity was with physicists because he became increasingly interested in establishing Synchronicity as a general principle of knowledge relevant for all the sciences and not limited to the study of man.

There is considerable point to this attempt on Jung's part. It reflected the conviction that grew in the background of the last period of his work that ultimately physics and psychology would come together.

He saw them as being joined by means of a master conception that would provide an inner guideline for working with the unity of the processes on both the physical and the psychological realms. In Jung's view, this linkage between the two fields is a realistic possibility because of the correspondence between the depth conception of the psyche and the physicist's view of the atom. If the energy locked into the depth of the atom can be released, may it not be possible also to release the energy that is in the depth of the human psyche?

Jung envisioned the dynamics of this as being distinctly feasible once the proper concepts have been formulated from both sides of the issue. He consciously turned his work in this direction, specifically believing that the form into which he had cast his system of depth psychology provided the underlying structure for a psychology that would eventually be capable of effecting a juncture with physics. Increasingly he became convinced that Synchronicity is the interpretive principle by which the main connection can be made. This is the primary reason why he preferred to present Synchronicity as a general principle in relation to all the realms of science and as not being confined to the human dimension of experience.

Jung's hope of connecting psychology and physics by means of the depth conception of the psyche and the principle of Synchronicity expressed a very large vision. At the moment it seems to be far from achievement, but the very thought of it is strongly suggestive and carries major implications. It opens far-reaching possibilities that will be of great value for our further consideration. The immediate point, however, is that this large vision caused Jung to direct his attention toward the broader possibilities of Synchronicity, and to present it as a general principle of science. He offered it as a means of interpreting the full range of natural phenomena, not limiting it to any specific field. In particular he did not restrict it to the category of phenomena that is the main area of synchronistic events, those in which the human psyche is one of the operant factors.

In fact, as he placed his emphasis on Synchronicity as a general principle of science, Jung tended to do so at the cost of documenting the presence of Synchronicity in the various areas of social experience, in parapsychic phenomena, and in the life history of individuals. The relevance of Synchronicity to these areas is of the largest consequence, but Jung barely indicates its possibilities. The role of Synchronicity in relation to the depth experiences of the psyche has tremendous significance for the study of man's life, and it certainly is essential as a base for the larger, more general consideration of the Synchronicity principle. Jung, however, placed himself in the position of underemphasizing the human base of Synchronicity. It seems that he became so fascinated by the larger possibility of connecting depth psychology with theoretical physics and with the natural sciences as a whole that he let his attention be drawn away from the human elements that needed to be studied. It was this oversight and the shifting of his attention that opened the way for the unclearness and misunderstandings in some of Jung's discussions of Synchronicity; and perhaps it was this also that made it possible for the Synchronicity trickster to play his jokes on Jung.

We have to consider both contexts, the larger and the more limited, if we are to appreciate the possibilities that Synchronicity opens for us. The key lies in understanding the nature of the processes that take place at the depths of the individual human being in relation not only to his immediate environment, but also in relation to all the universe at a given moment of time. The effective point of linkage is at the archetypal level. The specific archetypes that are active at the depth of an individual's existence are the means by which the general orderedness of the larger patterns of the macrocosm can come to specific expression at any moment of time. The archetypes are the vehicles by which the encompassing patterns of life are individualized in experience, and Synchronicity is the explanatory principle by which the chance and meaning of the intersection of these experiences in time may be recognized and comprehended.

This is the context in which we can understand Jung's statement that "The archetype *is* the introspectively recognizable form of *a priori* psychic orderedness."[1]

The archetypes alone hold the possibility of bringing about a connection via psychic experience be-

[1] Ibid., p. 516.

tween the individual human being and the noncausal ordering principle. On the other hand, since the archetype is itself an expression of the pattern, its "effect" on surrounding events is to draw them into conformity with the pervading principle. "If an external synchronistic process now associates itself with it, it falls into the same basic pattern—in other words, it too is 'ordered.' "[1] Thus, in those contingent situations *when* the process occurs, the pattern expressed in the archetype simply extends itself in terms of its prevailing characteristics, not causally but via the synchronistic ordering principle throughout the confluence of a given moment of time.

By considering the two-sidedness of the mediating role that the archetype plays, we can reach into the line of thinking that led Jung to the twofold aspect of the Synchronicity principle. In his formulation, it presents itself both as a large, comprehensive principle that pervades the macrocosm as a whole, and also as a narrower principle specifically pertaining to events in which the psyche is involved.

We have seen that Jung did not begin *a priori* with this double conception, but rather that it evolved in the course of his working with the hypothesis of Synchronicity. We must bear in mind that he developed his conception of Synchronicity while he was engaged in his primary work, the interpretation and therapeutic treatment of individuals. In that sense, Synchronicity is a by-product of his work as a psychotherapist.

[1] Ibid., p. 516, 517.

Its source material lies in the experiences of people's lives, as Jung observed them by the light of his depth psychology. This material suggested Synchronicity to him and drew the concept forth as he recognized that the depth study of individual human destiny requires an additional, more-than-causal perspective.

X Einstein and the Larger View

In its larger aspect, Jung presents Synchronicity as a principle equal in stature with causality, specifically formulated as a means of explaining the type of phenomena that may be attributed to the "acausal orderedness" found in the cosmos as a whole. In this respect, Synchronicity does not conflict with causality, but rather subsists side by side with it. He sees Synchronicity as a principle *sui generis,* in its own right and within its own terms.[1] Its value specifically is that it affords a means of dealing with those phenomena for which causality is not sufficient.

In Jung's statement of this aspect of his conception of Synchronicity, he gives as examples the phenomena of radium disintegration and the general areas of problems raised by discontinuities in physics. His claim is that since causal "laws" are merely statistical and not absolute by nature, they leave a range of events uncovered. This is the field where he offers

[1] Ibid., p. 483.

Synchronicity, not to controvert causality, but to balance and complete it. It is, however, in this area where Jung presents Synchronicity as a principle to be used by modern physics in reconstructing its view of the universe that he leaves the ground where the experience of his life and work have given him special competence.

Jung's venture beyond psychology into physics does indeed have its dangers. There have been other times when, in the nature of the pioneering thrust of his work, Jung has moved into areas beyond his immediate field of psychological competence. Those steps also have been precarious especially in their early stages. They have been vulnerable to criticism, not because they were taken carelessly, but because the intuitive visions by which they come are always ahead of the intellectual clarification that is eventually necessary to make them usable. Sometimes this intellectual clarification takes a long time in being achieved and has many pitfalls. Particularly in the case of so elusive a concept as Synchronicity, we may expect many difficulties to arise in the course of sharpening and refining it. We may hope, however, that as the process of reformulating the Synchronicity concept continues, it will always be done from a point of view that appreciates how large are the possibilities and implications that are opened by Jung's intuitive vision.

In its existential aspect, Synchronicity provides a means by which we can perceive and experience the correlations between the large patterns of the universe and the destiny of the individual. The medium for this is the depth of the psyche, and the vehicle for it is the archetypes when these are experienced at the deep psychoid ground of the Self. In this sense, Synchronicity helps us perceive the movement of life in the universe as that movement is reflected in the life of human beings.

As Jung sees Synchronicity in this narrower aspect, it "is only a particular instance of general acausal orderedness."[1] At this level, Synchronicity is much more specialized, and involves particularly those phenomena in which the psyche is a central factor. As Jung states it within this special and limited sense, "Synchronicity is a phenomenon that seems to be primarily connected with psychic conditions, that is to say, with processes in the unconscious."[2]

In Jung's lexicon, to speak of "processes in the unconscious," refers directly to the working of the archetypes and all their derivative phenomena. It takes us to another aspect of the idea already discussed, that the archetypes are mediators between the individual and the cosmos. In the more proximate sense, the archetypes draw that part of their physical (or social) surroundings to which they are *meaningfully related* into the pattern by which their own characteristics are defined. Synchronicity in its narrower definition means the coming together of a psychic event and a physical situation corresponding to it. As Jung puts

[1] Ibid., p. 516.
[2] Ibid., 511.

it, it means "the equivalence (*Gleichartigkeit*) of psychic and physical processes."[1]

The question of the relation between the mind and the body falls within this definition of Synchronicity. Several of the points that we have discussed in the foregoing presentation, from the abstract formulations of Leibniz to the laboratory work of parapsychology, may eventually, as they are understood within this context, lead to a resolution of the mind-body question. Large possibilities open in these areas of study. There is considerable research to be done in working out the specific forms and the active relationships between the archetypes and physical processes, as well as the synchronistic nature of the psychophysical processes in general. When empirical materials have been dealt with in this context, we may well find that at last we are in a position to develop a working hypothesis for studying the elusive but truly fundamental aspects of man's personal and social destiny.

In this perspective, we can see the major areas of enlarged understanding that open to us by means of the Synchronicity concept. We can also see the great tasks that this hypothesis has ahead of it. We are now, therefore, in a position where we can begin to consider what additional formulations and reformulations may be necessary to enable the Synchronicity principle to fulfill its promise.

In his 1946 address to the Eranos conference, where

[1] Ibid., p. 516.

he was primarily engaged in deepening and redefining his conception of the unconscious levels of the psyche, Jung dealt tangentially with a cluster of issues that are of great significance for refining the Synchronicity concept. That was a point in his thinking when Jung was working out the basic constructs that enabled him eventually to move from the theory of the psychoid to his formulation of Synchronicity. That is a point, therefore, where the primary lines in his thinking show through and enable us to see which concepts need to be reconsidered, and which steps in his thought process may need to be retraced.

In that discussion it becomes clear that Albert Einstein's theory of Relativity is a primary background both for Jung's own theory of Synchronicity and for his progressive reformulation of his theory of Archetypes. In writing about the relation of his work to physics, Jung makes hardly any reference to Einstein, preferring to place himself in relation to the thought of Nils Bohr. In our personal discussions, however, he told me of the years during the early part of the century when Einstein was working in Zurich and was a frequent visitor. Einstein would come for lunch, he said, and they would then become involved in long discussions.

At that point in his life, Jung was only at the beginning of his conceptual development, and he gave me the impression that he found it difficult to communicate to Einstein his new conceptions of the unconscious. He spoke, somewhat slightingly, of Einstein's having primarily an "analytical" mind. Jung was implying by this that he did not feel that Einstein had much aptitude for the symbolic dimensions of experience.

It is interesting in this regard to note that the recent opening of Einstein's private papers has disclosed that dreams and images played a very important role in Einstein's creative life. Those luncheon conversations may have been more fruitful than Jung realized, especially since we now know that Einstein possessed a keen sensitivity to the deep levels of the psyche. It may, at some later time, be very fruitful to study the relationship between Jung and Einstein more closely, particularly in view of Einstein's interest in Hindu/Buddhist thought and his later description of the archetypal qualities of the relativity concept.

While Jung may have had an important psychological effect on Einstein, the theory of Relativity became the base and starting point for his own thinking about Synchronicity. At several points he seems to have been consciously seeking to develop a concept that would be the equivalent of the relativity theory with the added dimension of the psyche.

Thus, in the published version of his Eranos lecture, Jung writes: "Physics has demonstrated, as plainly as could be wished, that in the realm of atomic magnitudes objective reality presupposes an observer, and that only on this condition is a satisfactory scheme of explanation possible. This means that a subjective element attaches to the physicist's world picture, and secondly that a connection necessarily exists between the psyche to be explained and the objective space-time continuum."[1] It may seem obvious for Jung to say in the nineteen-forties that there is a "subjective element" inherent in all man's knowledge of the physical world, no matter how objective the physicist may try to be; but to make room for that subjective factor had been part of Einstein's revolutionary contribution. The fact that the subjective condition of the observer is an additional factor in every situation is a primary factor in the conception of relativity theory. Nothing is ever final or complete, because there is always one more factor to be added. This is the element of subjectivity, the consciousness of the observer.

In the world view of relativity the universe is never static because there is always "one more" being added. If we recall now our discussion of the "changing lines" in the *I Ching*, we recognize the parallel of the "plus" factor. There is always the next increment of consciousness, and thus the perpetual presence of change in every situation in the universe. The theory of relativity applies this concept to the physical macrocosm, while the texts of the *I Ching* seek to apply it to the micrcocosm of individual destiny. There are the most seminal implications to be explored in the fact that the theory of relativity, which is one of the most profound products of the Western mind, parallels so closely the underlying principle of the *I Ching*,

[1] C. G. Jung. "On the Nature of the Psyche," in *Collected Works*, Vol. VIII, p. 230.

which ranks among the most profound creations of the Eastern mind.

Between the two, however, between relativity and the *I Ching*, there is a gap that needs to be crossed. To traverse it and to establish the connection between the two, is one of the primary goals of Synchronicity. That is the reason why Jung felt it necessary to become involved both in the general interpretation of the physical macrocosm and in the specific study of the psychological microcosm. To link the apparent opposites of life in a meaningful formulation is the underlying purpose of the Synchronicity principle. Even though it has not achieved this completely, the fact is that in its contents Synchronicity inherently combines the opposites of the outer and the inner, the physical situation and the psychic event.

The central problem that Jung sought to resolve is the question of how the physical and the psychical are connected. Starting with the awareness given by Einsteinian relativity, it was clear to him that causality in its usual definition is not the means by which the connection can be comprehended. In some way, it seemed to him, the answer is to be found not along the path of causality but by means of some conception of a *continuum*. The nature of this continuum was not clear to him. In fact, Jung stated it as a fact that both a "physical continuum" and a "psychic continuum" are inherently "inconceivable," since we can make no picture or image of what such a continuum would be.

154

"Nevertheless," Jung wrote, "the relative or partial-identity of psyche and physical continuum is of the greatest importance theoretically, because it brings with it a tremendous simplification by bridging over the seeming incommensurability between the physical world and the psychic, not of course in any concrete way, but from the physical side by means of mathematical equations, and from the psychological side by means of empirically derived postulates—archetypes—whose content, if any, cannot be represented to the mind."[1] Here we see the encompassing vision by which Jung conceived of drawing the physical and psychic realms of the cosmos together. The physical world is given its order and patterning by means of mathematics, while the comparable structuring of the world of the psyche is brought about by the archetypes. This is the *ordering* quality of the archetypes of which we have spoken.

"Archetypes," Jung says, "manifest themselves through their ability to organize images and ideas." In this sense, what Jung speaks of as *archetypes* are specific organizing factors that operate on the realm of the psyche. They carry definite patterns and modes by which they organize the contents of the psyche but, as Jung points out, their patterning is "always an unconscious process which cannot be detected until afterwards."[2]

This fundamental, as well as inconvenient, aspect of the archetypes is very important to bear in mind.

[1] Ibid., p. 231.
[2] Ibid., p. 231.

The fact that the presence and activity of an arche-type becomes visible and can be recognized only *after the fact* means that activation and expression of an archetype cannot be planned in advance. If it is to be brought about, it can only be by means of the most subtle techniques. In any case, archetypes can-not be predicted in advance with respect to the spon-taneous events of life. That is a primary reason why it is so difficult to mark off and delineate any particu-lar archetypes. It is very misleading to identify specific archetypes by name, although the archetypal effect, i.e., the interior ordering and structuring of the psyche that archetypes bring about, is definite and visible.

This is the reason why, in my Eranos lecture of 1966,[1] I made the point that in the final analysis it is incorrect to speak of *archetypes* as nouns, if we are implying by that that each has a specific and individ-ual existence. It is a correct description, however, to use the term as an adjective, for then we are speaking of the general *archetypal* effect that is brought about by the organizational quality of archetypes.

It is this general *archetypal* factor that Jung is re-ferring to, and that he sets side by side with the math-ematical factor in physics. Each serves as an ordering factor within its own realm, and the two together complement one another in presenting the psycho-physical universe from both sides.

[1] Ira Progoff. *The Man Who Transforms Consciousness: The Inner Myths of Martin Buber, Paul Tillich, and C. G. Jung.* Eranos Jahrbuch, 1966, Schöpfung und Gestaltung, Rhein-Verlag, Zurich, 1967, p. 99.

In addition, Jung points out that the archetypes "have a nonpsychic aspect." This is the *psychoid* aspect of archetypes of which we have spoken. It is the primal form of the contents of the human psyche when they have not yet become specifically psychological, or when they have dropped down from the psychological level to touch the undifferentiated state of nature. Here in the *psychoid* aspect of archetypes that is reached through the *abaissement* of the mental level, the events that express the principle of Synchronicity come about. At this point, the psychological has become deeper than the psyche. It has become nonpsychic, and therefore no longer separated from the physical aspect of nature. When the psychic and the physical are no longer differentiated from one another, a continuum is established in which synchronistic events can come to pass.

With this statement we can see the full conception and the view of the universe within which Jung sees the principle of Synchronicity to be operating. It is indeed a full world view. Seeing this, we are in a better position to appreciate the reasons for which Jung insisted on emphasizing the larger aspects of the Synchronicity principle, despite the difficulty he encountered in describing it, and despite the fact that he was aware of the many specific areas of personal and social experiences in which it could be applied.

He felt the great importance, despite its subtle and elusive difficulty, of communicating this large view of the universe in which the Synchronicity principle has a place beside the relativity principle. As a result of the intricate exposition through which we have just passed, we can recognize that this was Jung's private perception of what he was doing. He felt that what he was developing in his theory of Synchronicity was a principle equal to, and commensurate with, the theory of relativity developed by his old friend Einstein. His theory had the added merit of including the dimension of the psyche in a comprehensive view of the universe.

This was Jung's private view of what he was doing in working with his Synchronicity principle. The trouble was that if he had said this in just so many words, he would have seemed to be claiming much too much for himself and could easily have been accused of vanity and an undue intellectual ambition. He had indeed been unfairly accused of this in the past when his conceptions were not appreciated by unfriendly critics. Realizing now the subjective view that Jung held of the magnitude of what he was seeking to do where the Synchronicity principle is concerned, we can understand also why he was so often irritated and frustrated in working with it. His vision was so rich and essentially valid, but he could not reduce it to a form that he could communicate, and he could not say the things that needed to be said in order to reflect his vision. Thus the goal eluded him and left him irritable. Nonetheless, he did the basic groundwork and developed it as far as he could. That was the foundation that he provided for another generation to build upon.

XI From Synchronicity to the Transcausal

We come now to the point in our study where we can begin to raise the question of what further formulation or refinement of concept can assist the Synchronicity principle in establishing itself and in being taken further to fulfill its promise. A first clue in this direction comes from a footnote that Jung inserted in the 1946 Eranos lecture from which we have been quoting. "Synchronicity," he said, "a term for which I am to blame, is an unsatisfactory expression in so far as it only takes account of time phenomena."[1]

[1] This statement appears as a footnote in Jung's original published version of his Eranos Lectures under the title, "Der Geist der Psychologie." See Eranos Jahrbuch, 1946, Geist und Natur, Rhein-Verlag, Zurich, 1947, p. 485. It also appears in the translation of that essay published in the series of selected papers given at the Eranos Conferences. See Joseph Campbell, ed., "Papers from the Eranos Yearbooks," Vol. I, Spirit and Nature. Jung's essay is there printed under its original title, "The Spirit of Psychology," p. 371ff. The footnote with the comment on Synchronicity appears there on p. 440. It has, however, not been included in the version of that essay published in the *Collected Works*, which there appears under the title, "On the Nature of the Psyche."

Jung went on to say that he felt the term, Synchronicity, to be inadequate because, in referring only to time phenomena, it ignores all other types of events and experiences that may be relevant. He mentions specifically that space phenomena should also be included, as in the case of events described under the heading of "spatial clairvoyance." Implicitly, in making this point about the insufficiency of Synchronicity as a term to describe the fullness of the phenomena involved in it, Jung was indicating that other aspects than time may play an important role in it. In fact, as his work on Synchronicity proceeded, the factor that increasingly came to the fore is the constellative quality of the archetypes. Repeatedly we have seen that the factor of integrative orderedness is of primary importance in synchronistic phenomena, and yet it is not reflected at all in the term, nor in any part of the nomenclature that Jung developed. This is one major point where a sharper formulation with a more specific terminology may be helpful in extending the work.

We have seen Jung's general conception of Synchronicity as a principle *sui generis,* a principle in its own right inherent in the cosmos, and comparable to causality. In Jung's conception, causality and Synchronicity stand in a balancing and complementary relationship to each other. We have seen also that while the co-occurrence of events in time is a major aspect of Synchronicity, it is not its definitive characteristic. What is more important, co-occurrence is a descriptive rather than an effective factor. It does not in itself bring synchronistic events into being. The essence of Synchronicity is to be found in the fact that Synchronicity carries a principle of orderedness that occurs in the universe regardless of causal connections and beyond space and time. Synchronicity may occur in the universe on all its levels, but implicit in its definition as involving *meaningful* coincidences is the presence of an *organ of meaning* that is an inherent part of each synchronistic event.

One of Jung's important contributions in this regard lies in his pointing out that such an organ of meaning is not necessarily the conscious mind or the intellect, as would be the case in David Hume's perception of causality, or as would equally be the case for the scientific observer in Einsteinian physics. Jung's depth psychology enables him to see that the organ of meaning may be operating at a level much deeper than consciousness or intellect. The meaning may, in fact, be experienced at the unconscious level of personal emotion, or, beyond that, at a truly archetypal depth. At the point where an archetypal factor becomes involved in a situation, something more active than the conscious mind of an observer enters the picture. It is also a more active factor than the presence of an unconscious emotion. The archetypal element becomes an effective factor in the situation because it serves to recrystallize and reconstitute the situation as a whole. As the effective factor, it creates a new situation; and it becomes the core of the new quality of orderedness that permeates and characterizes the new situation as it exists *across time.*

This working of the archetypal element in a situation cannot be encompassed in any of the usual
definitions of causality. It is not causal, but rather
recrystallizing and restructuring. It reconstitutes a situation across time without respect to the causal connections within it, without respect to boundaries of
space, and without respect to any directive factor of
the conscious mind. It moves across causality, and its
effects are beyond causality. To this degree, the archetypal element that recrystallizes the unity of a situation across time is a *transcausal factor*.

Wherever it emerges, the *transcausal factor* sets its
stamp upon a synchronistic event. We have seen that
the basic elements in a synchronistic situation are two
or more separate lines of continuous, causally connected events. Each line of events has its own chain
of causality within it, but the lines are not causally
related to one another. They are altogether separate
and disconnected until an additional factor enters the
situation. This additional factor involves meaning, or
interest, or involvement, or other intense psychic concern sufficient to bring about a partial *abaissement* of
the mental level.

In the course of that *abaissement,* archetypal factors at the depth of the psyche are activated in such a
way as to reach *across* the causally unrelated lines of
causation and draw them together in a striking and
significant event that transcends the causality of the
events that preceded it. The archetypal element serves
to crystallize the essence of each line of causality so
that it draws them together in a new constellation

bearing the stamp and the interest of the activated archetype. This is how the *meaningfulness* is brought about in what Jung calls *meaningful coincidence.* It is the restructuring of situations across time and beyond causality in terms of the reordering element at the depth of the psyche.

The manner in which this meaningful restructuring takes place is elusive, primarily because it cannot be brought about by deliberate purpose. Atmospheres can be set up in which it becomes more possible for it to happen, but no definite script can be written in advance, since causality is not involved in it. When the reconstellative element becomes active, events and awarenesses come together in a way that reaches across time and space, and that goes beyond causality. Synchronicity is thus brought into play by means of a specific ordering factor that moves across and beyond causality. This is the *transcausal factor* that makes synchronistic events possible.

Jung himself did not use the term transcausal, but the deeper we move into his thinking on Synchronicity, the clearer it becomes that this is the core of his concept. The operation of the Synchronicity principle depends upon a factor that moves *across and beyond causality.* As it does this, it reconstellates the components of a given moment of time and thus brings forth new and meaningful events. The conception of a transcausal factor is thus inherent in the Synchronicity principle, and is specifically the active element in it. The indication is, therefore, that as we proceed in using Jung's formulation of Synchronicity as an hypothesis for further research, the transcausal factor will be the most fruitful place for us to direct our attention.

It is clear that the next necessary step in working with the Synchronicity principle is to establish a systematic program of research by which we can identify and describe in detail the occurrence of synchronistic events in the life of man. There is tremendous importance in our recognizing the implications of Synchronicity as an interpretive principle of universal processes, side by side with causality and relativity. When the day comes that Jung's vision can be fulfilled and atomic physics can be united with depth psychology, it will be a moment of tremendous magnitude in man's spiritual history. Toward that day, there is considerable specific research to be done, and the data for that research is to be found in the events of human experience. Not only is this the material that is most readily available to us, but Synchronicity has a special contribution to make to our understanding of the nuances of human destiny, both in personal life and in history. This is the point where Synchronicity links with Teilhard de Chardin's conception of the *Noosphere* and supplements it with an essential dimension of knowledge. It is also the point at which the additional conception of *Transcausality* becomes the pivotal factor in enabling us to translate the abstract principle of Synchronicity into an understanding of the riddles of human existence.

Recognizing the transcausal factor to be the primary effective element in synchronistic events gives us a criterion by which we can gather and screen our empirical data. Up to this point in the study of Synchronicity, descriptions have tended to be generalized, and sometimes impressionistic. In developing his case of Synchronicity, Jung tended to use as his evidence events that had occurred in the course of his psychotherapeutic experience. He told, for example, of a person having a dream of a strange bird or an unusual insect, and in the moment of the telling of that dream, a bird or an insect of that species appeared. We know, in a similar way, of examples of life situations in which a person seeking to become an artist takes his meager savings and lives in a garret, hoping he can sell a painting before his money is gone. No paintings are sold and the money is exhausted. In the moment, however, that the person is giving up on his art in despair, a telegram arrives saying that an unknown relative has died and left a small inheritance. These are the somewhat impressionistic instances of "meaningful coincidence" that are the more common examples of Synchronicity. These involve the significant coming together of two lines of events each of which has its own causal background while neither is causally related to the other. The question at issue is the nature of the *transcausal factor* involved in such situations.

Many striking events of this kind occur throughout the range of human experience. They are the dramatic examples, and Jung referred to them in order to emphasize his point. Now that we have recognized the presence of the transcausal factor, however, we are in a position to identify more definitely the type of information that is relevant for our research. As we do this, we shall very likely find that the events in which the principle of Synchronicity is expressed are much more numerous than we have realized. They occur in small, unobserved ways all through our lives. They affect our personal destiny in ways that we do not recognize because we are not perceiving them by the light of the synchronistic principle. The reason that we have not observed them before is that we did not know what we were looking for. Now, as we place our direct focus upon the presence of the transcausal factor in synchronistic events, we have a guideline that should enable us to frame new hypotheses and find additional clues to the nature of synchronistic events.

There are numerous specific questions to which we are seeking answers in terms of Synchronicity and the transcausal factor. What are the varieties of synchronistic phenomena? In what forms do they appear? What are their particular characteristics? What are the factors that initiate them or give them their crystallized form? Are there specific characteristics by which we can recognize synchronistic events as they are preparing to occur?

What are the processes by which synchronistic events take place? Is it correct to speak of *process* where the principle involved is a noncausal one? Do we require new terms to replace concepts like *process* in the light of Synchronicity and the transcausal factor? Or will it be sufficient to define these terms more closely and in new ways?

Is it possible for individuals to develop a greater capacity for bringing synchronistic events to pass? And is there any advantage in doing so? Is it possible to develop a greater sensitivity to the operation of the principle of Synchronicity? Can we develop means of being in closer relationship to it? And is there any special value in achieving this, if it can be done?

The first step toward answering these questions, and the others that will arise in relation to them, lies in describing the variety of synchronistic events with step-by-step objective factuality. It is necessary for us to recapitulate and examine closely events like the throwing of the *I Ching* coins, psychophysical changes, healings, and religious transformations, striking events in the life destiny of individuals and also of society. By retracing what takes place in occurrences of this kind, we shall be able to understand a great deal more about the human being as individual, and the individual as an agent of history. The vantage point of Synchronicity gives us access to those subtle aspects of human experience that are dealt with so elusively in the *I Ching* and in comparable ancient, esoteric texts.

For the purposes of carrying this research further, we can draw upon areas of study where the work already in progress has involved the gathering of data that is relevant for Synchronicity. Two such areas are part of my experience. One is *the comparative study of lives,* as it has been conducted for a number of years at the Graduate Institute for Research in Depth Psychology. The other is the data created and collected as part of the *Journal Feedback* method of personal growth conducted by Dialogue House.

The first area of work, the comparative study of lives, involves the close recapitulation of the inner development of individuals through all the cycles of their experience. To examine the continuity of experience in the lives of persons of all types, of all levels of success and failure, and of all cultures and social positions, serves many purposes of human understanding. Without seeking them, we find that a substantial number of synchronistic experiences appear in the course of such studies. One specific hypothesis that is worth investigating is whether the lives of those individuals who can be classified as "creative persons" show a particular tendency toward the occurrence of synchronistic events. If this turns out to be verified in any degree, the implications may be of great importance.

The second area of work that offers a natural and plentiful source of data for the study of Synchronicity is that of the *Intensive Journal* program of personal growth conducted by Dialogue House. The Dialogue House method of Journal keeping has a purpose that is quite distinct from that of recording experiences that fall within the categories of Synchronicity. Its goal is primarily to assist the process of individual development throughout the continuity of a person's life. In the course of this work, however, many unplanned experiences that meet Jung's criteria of Synchronicity do in fact take place. These experiences are all the more significant since they occur spontaneously. They thus indicate the unnoticed prevalence of synchronistic phenomena in the ordinary course of a human life. The data that is accumulating in the Dialogue House records is a valuable and unanticipated by-product of its special method of personal growth.

There is a second reason for which the Dialogue House program brings about synchronistic events, and it is of more fundamental significance than the more neutral fact of disciplined Journal keeping. This involves the basic nature of the specific method used in the Dialogue House Intensive Journal program. In the method of *Journal Feedback,* the primary procedures are directed toward bringing about a progressive deepening of atmosphere both in the group experience and in the individual's use of the Intensive Journal. The use of the techniques of *Process Meditation* within this program of personal growth also contributes significantly to the deepening of the atmosphere.

The process of deepening the quality of group and personal experience is of the greatest importance for establishing an environment in which synchronistic experiences can occur and for increasing the individual's sensitivity to them. Deepening the atmosphere assists in achieving what we have seen to be two of the main factors in Jung's understanding of synchronistic events. The first is that it brings about the condition of *abaissement du niveau mental,* the lowering of the mental level. The second is that it activates and sensitizes the *psychoid* level of the personality, the depth beneath the transpersonal *collective uncon-*

scious. Jung's description of the *psychoid* depth of the psyche in 1946 made it possible for him to proceed in articulating his conception of Synchronicity. That, in turn, has made it possible to recognize the *transcausal factor* as it is present in Synchronicity, and to proceed to an understanding of synchronistic events in a way that opens the possibility of stimulating them and bringing them about.

To a significant degree, procedures of this kind are present within the Dialogue House program of Journal Feedback. Not only the specific techniques but, even more, the underlying atmosphere in which the work is conducted serves to bring about synchronistic events. This is true even though the program was originally developed with a quite different purpose in mind and is still primarily directed toward the work of the creative development of individuals. As a result of this work, however, a significant store of synchronistic data has been gathered over the years of Dialogue House experience. This data is available now and is waiting to be used in further research.

There is a synchronistic event that occurred in the life of Abraham Lincoln that may say a great deal to us about the nature of Synchronicity and its future. During his early years, as we know, Lincoln found himself in a very difficult and conflicting situation. He had intimations of the fact that there was a meaningful work for him to do in the world. He realized, however, that that work would require him to develop his intellect and to acquire professional skills. In conflict with these subjective feelings was the fact that, in Lincoln's frontier environment, intellectual tools for professional study were very difficult to find. He had reason to believe that his hopes would never be fulfilled.

One day a stranger came to Lincoln with a barrel full of odds and ends. He said that he was in need of money and that he would be much obliged if Lincoln would help him out by giving him a dollar for the barrel. The contents, he said, were not of much value; they were some old newspapers and things of that sort. But the stranger needed the dollar very badly. The story tells us that Lincoln, with his characteristic kindness, gave the man a dollar for the barrel even though he could not imagine any use that he would have for its contents. Some time later, when he went to clear out the barrel, he found that it contained almost a complete edition of Blackstone's *Commentaries*. It was the chance, or synchronistic, acquisition of these books that enabled Lincoln to become a lawyer and eventually to embark on his career in politics.

There was one line of continuous causality working within the life of Lincoln, stirring his intimations of destiny, and filling him with the despair of living in a limited and difficult environment. At the same time, there was the causal continuity in the life of the stranger who came upon hard times and had to sell whatever belongings he could find for a dollar. The two lines of events had no causal connection linking them. At a significant moment of time, however, they came together. This was the working of the transcausal factor in Synchronicity, as it brought about its unanticipated results.

Lincoln's purchase of the barrel with his inadvertent acquisition of Blackstone's *Commentaries* is an instance of the occurrence of synchronistic events in the life of man. It is an example of Synchronicity, but it may serve as a symbol for us of how Synchronicity will eventually give us her riches of knowledge. It will be in unexpected ways and where we least expect to find them. But if, like Lincoln, we are true to the integrity of the moment, there is some reason to believe that the intuition that was Jung's will become a knowledge for all of us.

Bibliography

Barnett, Lincoln. *The Universe and Dr. Einstein.* rev. ed. New York: The New American Library of World Literature, Inc., 1950.

Brain, W. Russell. *Mind, Perception and Science.* Oxford: Blackwell Scientific Publications, 1951.

Bucke, Richard Maurice. *Cosmic Consciousness.* New York: University Books, Inc., 1961.

Campbell, Joseph, ed. *Spirit and Nature.* Vol. 1. Papers from the Eranos Yearbooks. New York: Pantheon Books Inc., 1954.

_____ *The Mysteries.* Vol. 2. Papers from the Eranos Yearbooks. New York: Pantheon Books Inc., 1955.

_____ *Man and Time.* Vol. 3. Papers from the Eranos Yearbooks. New York: Pantheon Books Inc., 1957.

_____ *Spiritual Disciplines.* Vol. 4. Papers from the Eranos Yearbooks. New York: Pantheon Books Inc., 1960.

Cassirer, Ernst. *An Essay on Man.* New Haven: Yale University Press, 1944.

de Chardin, Pierre Teilhard. *The Phenomenon of Man.* New York: Harper & Brothers, 1959.

_____ *The Divine Milieu.* New York: Harper & Brothers, 1960.

_____ *The Appearance of Man.* New York: Harper & Row, Publishers, Inc., 1965.

de Lubac, Henri. *Teilhard de Chardin: The Man and his Meaning.* Translated by René Hague. New York: The New American Library, Inc., 1967.

Dubos, René. *The Torch of Life.* New York: Pocket Books, Inc., 1963.

Eliade, Mircea. *Birth and Rebirth.* Translated by Willard R. Trask. New York: Harper & Brothers, 1958.

_____ *Patterns in Comparative Religion.* Translated by Rosemary Sheed. New York: Sheed and Ward, Inc., 1958.

_____ *Cosmos and History: The Myth of the Eternal Return.* Translated by Willard R. Trask. New York: Harper & Brothers, 1959.

_____ *Myths, Dreams and Mysteries.* Translated by Philip Mairet. New York: Harper & Brothers, 1960.

_____ *Images & Symbols: Studies in Religious Symbolism.* Translated by Philip Mairet. New York: Sheed & Ward, Inc., 1961.

_____ *Shamanism: Archaic Techniques of Ecstasy.* Translated by Willard R. Trask. New York: Bollingen Fdn., 1964.

Evans-Wentz, W. Y. *The Tibetan Book of the Dead.* 2nd ed. London: Geoffrey Cumberlege, Oxford University Press, 1949.

Ford, Arthur. *Nothing So Strange.* New York: Paperback Library, Inc., 1968.

Frankfurt, Harry G. ed. *Leibniz: A Collection of Critical Essays.* New York: Doubleday & Company, Inc., 1972.

Fuller, John G. *The Great Soul Trail.* New York: The Macmillan Company, 1969.

Garrett, Eileen J. *Telepathy: In Search of a Lost Faculty.* New York: Creative Age Press, Inc., 1945.

———————— *Awareness.* New York: Creative Age Press, Inc. 1945.

———————— *Adventures in the Supernormal: A Personal Memoir.* New York: Garrett Publications, Inc., 1949.

Heard, Gerald. *The Five Ages of Man.* New York: The Julian Press, Inc., 1963.

———————— *Pain, Sex and Time.* New York: Harper & Brothers, 1939.

Hegel, G. W. F. *The Phenomenology of Mind.* Translated by J. B. Baillie. New York: Harper & Row, Publishers, Inc., 1967.

Hume, David. *Hume's Moral and Political Philosophy.* Edited by Henry D. Aiken. New York: Hafner Publishing Company, 1948.

Huxley, Aldous. *The Devils of Loudun.* London: Chatto & Windus, 1952.

I Ching: or Book of Changes. The Richard Wilhelm translation rendered into English by Cary F. Baynes. Foreword by C. G. Jung. 3rd ed. Princeton: Princeton University Press, 1950.

I Ching. Translated by James Legge. 2nd ed. New York: Dover Publications, Inc. 1963.

James, William. *Varieties of Religious Experience.* New York: Random House, Inc., 1902.

Jung, C. G. *Contributions to Analytical Psychology.* Translated by H. G. and Cary F. Baynes. London: Routledge & Kegan Paul Limited, 1928.

———————— *Synchronicity: An Acausal Connecting Principle.* in Jung, C. G. & Pauli, W. *The Interpretation of Nature and the Psyche.* New York: Pantheon Books Inc., 1955.

———————— *Synchronicity: An Acausal Connecting Principle.* Collected Works. Vol. 8. in *The Structure and Dynamics of the Psyche.* New York: Pantheon Books Inc., 1960.

———————— *Synchronizitat als ein Prinzip Akausaler Zusammenhänge.* in Jung, C. G. & Pauli, W. *Naturerklärung und Psyche.* Zurich: Rascher Verlag, 1952.

———————— *Psychology and Religion: West and East.* Collected Works of C. G. Jung. Vol. 11. Translated by R. F. C. Hull. New York: Pantheon Books Inc., 1959.

———————— *The Archetypes and the Collective Unconscious.* Collected Works. Vol. 9, part 1. Translated by R. F. C. Hull. New York: Pantheon Books Inc., 1959.

———————— *Aion: Researches into the Phenomenology of the Self.* Collected Works. Vol. 9, part 2. Translated by R. F. C. Hull. New York: Pantheon Books Inc., 1959.

Bibliography

_____ *The Structure and Dynamics of the Psyche.* Collected Works. Vol. 8. Translated by R. F. C. Hull. New York: Pantheon Books Inc., 1960.

Laotzu: The Way of Life. An American version by Witter Bynner. New York: The John Day Company, 1964.

Lao Tzu. A new translation of the Tao Tê Ching by R. B. Blakney. New York: The New American Library, 1955.

Lao Tzu. Translated by D. C. Lau. Baltimore: Penguin Books, 1963.

Levin, Meyer. *Classic Hassidic Tales.* New York: The Citadel Press, 1966.

McDougall, William. *Body and Mind: A History and Defense of Animism.* London: Methuen & Co., Ltd., 1911.

_____ *The Group Mind.* New York: G. P. Putnam's Sons, 1920.

_____ *Outline of Abnormal Psychology.* New York: Charles Scribner's Sons, 1926.

McNeill, John T. *A History of the Cure of Souls.* New York: Harper & Brothers, 1951.

Meerloo, Joost A. M. *The Two Faces of Man.* New York: International Universities Press, Inc., 1954.

Meyer, R. W. *Leibnitz and the Seventeenth-Century Revolution.* Hamburg: Joachim Heitmann and Company, 1948. Translated by J. P. Stern. England: Bowes and Bowes, Publishers Limited, 1952.

Neumann, Erich. *Art and the Creative Unconscious.* Translated by Ralph Manheim. New York: Pantheon Books Inc., 1959.

Otto, Rudolf. *The Idea of the Holy.* Translated by John W. Harvey. New York: Oxford University Press, 1958.

Ouspensky, P. D. *Strange Life of Ivan Osokin.* London: Faber and Faber.

Radin, Paul. *The Road of Life and Death.* New York: Pantheon Books Inc., 1945.

_____ *The World of Primitive Man.* New York: Henry Schuman, Inc., 1953.

_____ *The Trickster.* with commentaries by Karl Kerenyi & C. G. Jung. New York: Philosophical Library Inc., 1956.

Reiser, Oliver L. *Cosmic Humanism.* Cambridge: Schenkman Publishing Co., 1966.

Rhine, Joseph Banks. *New World of the Mind.* New York: William Sloane Associates, 1953.

Rhine, J. B. ed. *Progress in Parapsychology.* Durham: The Parapsychology Press, 1971.

Royce, Josiah. *The Sources of Religious Insight.* New York: Charles Scribner's Sons, 1912.

Sinnott, Edmund W. *The Biology of the Spirit.* New York: Viking Press, Inc., 1955.

Siu, R. G. H. *The Tao of Science*. Cambridge: The M.I.T. Press. 1964.

Sorokin, Pitirim A. *Altruistic Love*. Boston: Beacon Press, 1950.

Speaight, Robert. *The Life of Teilhard de Chardin*. New York: Harper & Row, Publishers, Inc., 1967.

Stephenson, Nathaniel W. *Lincoln*. Indianapolis: The Bobbs-Merrill Company, 1922.

Stern, Karl. *The Third Revolution*. New York: Harcourt, Brace and Co., 1954.

Stern, Philip Van Doren, ed. *The Life and Writings of Abraham Lincoln*. New York: Random House, Inc., 1940.

Sugrue, Thomas. *There is a River*. New York: Dell Publishing Co. Inc., 1961.

Thomas, Benjamin P. *Abraham Lincoln*. New York: Alfred A. Knopf, 1952.

Trowbridge, George. *Swedenborg: Life and Teaching*. New York: Swedenborg Fdn. Inc., 1962.

Veblen, Thorstein. *The Instinct of Workmanship*. New York: Viking Press, Inc., 1914, 1937.

_____ *The Place of Science in Modern Civilization*. New York: Viking Press, Inc., 1919, 1942.

Weatherhead, Leslie D. *Psychology, Religion and Healing*. rev. ed. Nashville: Abingdon Press, 1951.

Weizsäcker, C. F. v. *The World View of Physics*. London: Routledge & Kegan Paul Ltd., 1952.

Wheeler, L. Richmond. *Vitalism: Its History & Validity*. London: H. F. & G. Witherby Ltd., 1939.

Whitehead, Alfred North. *Science and the Modern World*. New York: The New American Library of World Literature, Inc., 1948.

Wiener, Philip P., ed. *Leibniz: Selections*. New York: Charles Scribner's Sons, 1951.

Wilhelm, Hellmut. *Change: Eight Lectures on the I Ching*. Translated by Cary F. Baynes. New York: Harper & Row, Publishers, Inc., 1960.

Wilhelm, Richard, translator with a European commentary by C. G. Jung. *The Secret of the Golden Flower*. London: Kegan Paul, Trench, Trubner & Co., Ltd., 1931.

Zaehner, R. C. *Matter and Spirit*. New York: Harper & Row, Publishers, Inc., 1963.

Zimmer, Heinrich. *Myths and Symbols in Indian Art and Civilization*. ed. by Joseph Campbell. New York: Pantheon Books Inc., 1946.

 **For more than thirty years, the Julian Press has been a pioneer, publishing classic books in the fields of philosophy, psychology, metaphysics, spiritualism, and Eastern studies authored by the most original thinkers and writers in their respective areas of expertise.**

If you enjoyed this Julian Press title, here is a list of other books of special interest:

☐ *Reincarnation: A New Horizon in Science, Religion, and Society* by Sylvia Cranston and Carey Williams
A comprehensive, readable guide to contemporary past-life research. "Unique in its ability to pull together all aspects of the theory."—*BOOKLIST*
554968. $16.95 hardcover

☐ *The Evil Eye* by Frederick Thomas Elsworthy
The classic study of man's ancient and universal belief in the eye's power to cast malignant spells. "A scholarly work of lasting importance."
—*LIBRARY JOURNAL* 559714. $7.95 paper

☐ *Tantra: The Yoga of Sex* by Omar Garrison
A complete guidebook to the theory and practice of harnessing the power of sexual union with Tantra Yoga. 549484. $8.95 paper

☐ *Reincarnation: The Phoenix Fire Mystery* compiled and edited by Joseph Head and S. L. Cranston
A stimulating, in-depth look at how the world's greatest minds throughout history have viewed the concept of reincarnation. "Fascinating and moving to read."—*LOS ANGELES TIMES* 561018. $12.95 paper

☐ *The Center of the Cyclone* by John C. Lilly, M.D.
"Dr. John Lilly's spiritual autobiography is a bold effort to convey his theory of the superconscious, and of the meaning of expanded awareness. . . . moving, mysterious, even beautiful."—*PUBLISHERS WEEKLY* 556146. $7.95 paper

☐ *Communication Between Man and Dolphin* by John C. Lilly, M.D.
The culmination of Dr. John Lilly's groundbreaking research into mankind's potential for talking with other species. "Fascinating reading."
—*WASHINGTON POST* 565641. $10.95 paper

☐ *Programming and Metaprogramming in the Human Biocomputer* by John C. Lilly, M.D.
Dr. John Lilly's report on his controversial experiments and investigations into the workings of the brain and the process of thought. 52757X. $10.95 paper

By the year 2000, 2 out of 3 Americans could be illiterate.

It's true.

Today, 75 million adults...about one American in three, can't read adequately. And by the year 2000, U.S. News & World Report envisions an America with a literacy rate of only 30%.

Before that America comes to be, you can stop it...by joining the fight against illiteracy today.

Call the Coalition for Literacy at toll-free **1-800-228-8813** and volunteer.

**Volunteer
Against Illiteracy.
The only degree you need
is a degree of caring.**

Ad Council Coalition for Literacy